The
Teddy
Bear

For Jinny

*I would like to thank the following people who helped me
in many different ways with the compilation of this
anthology, especially those who let me draw their bears:*
Marion Waller, Deborah Brown, Mary Hillier, Jenny
Shapeero, Pippa Draper, Dorothy Theobalds, Anna Awdry,
Dr Ian Christie, Judy Stovell, Michael Burden, Jock Murray,
James Roose-Evans, Tina Woolley, Lucy Maxwell-Stewart,
Joan G. Robinson, Lucy Hick, Claudia Waddams, James
Theobalds, Col. Bob Henderson, The Bethnal Green
Museum of Childhood, The Royal Military Academy,
Sandhurst, The House of Nisbet, Jackie Reid of Kent County
Library and the staff of East Sussex County Library, Hastings,
especially Pauline Crouch and Joanne Webb. Lastly, my
thanks to Rosemary Lanning, without whose guidance and
indefatigable perseverance this book would not have been
realised.

The Teddy Bear

An Anthology Compiled and Illustrated by
PRUE THEOBALDS

Prue Theobalds

Blackie

First published in 1988 by
Blackie and Son Ltd
7 Leicester Place, London WC2H 7BP

British Library Cataloguing in Publication Data

The teddy bear.
  1. Teddy bears – Juvenile fiction
  2. Children's literature, English
  I. Theobalds, Prue
  820.8'0355   PZ5

  ISBN 0-216-92393-X

Designed by Malcolm Smythe

Studio work by Keith Shannon

Typeset in Cheltenham ITC Light by
Dorchester Typesetting Group

Printed in GDR

CONTENTS

B was once a little bear,
> Beary!
> Wary!
> Hairy!
> Beary!
> Taky cary!
> Little bear!

EDWARD LEAR

Introduction

In compiling this anthology I have tried to show a representative selection from the great mass of material that has been written on the subject of teddy bears from the earliest years of the century until the present day. The book is presented in a loosely chronological pattern and does not necessarily include all the well-known characters of the teddy bear world, but rather pieces that are either historically interesting, different from each other, or have appeal for me personally. One of the main aims of the book is to show portraits of the real bears that have inspired, or had relevance to, the various writings. The drawings throughout are of real teddy bears of many different ages, nationalities and characters, as are the pieces they illustrate. Although this is a personal selection, I hope that everyone will find something to enjoy whatever their age or level of teddy bear interest.

In the Beginning . . .

The first toy bears as such were certainly made during the nineteenth century; many a Victorian nursery would have been familiar with them, either on wheels or as performing bears with a muzzle and chain; these were often known as Bruin. By 1880, in a small town in Germany, a crippled seamstress called Margarete Steiff was experimenting with soft toys and made a small, felt elephant which proved so successful that she made a whole range of animals and in 1893 exhibited them at the

Leipzig Toy Fair where they were an immediate success. Her nephew, Richard, joined the firm after completing his sculpture studies at Stuttgart and produced some drawings of a particularly engaging performing bear. He was very keen that Margarete should make a soft toy bear in mohair with jointed arms and legs. At first she did not like the idea because the mohair was difficult to obtain, but she eventually produced a bear and named him 'Friend Petz'. There was little immediate interest in the new toy but then, on the other side of the Atlantic, something happened that was destined to make changes for 'Friend Petz' and the name of Steiff for ever.

In November 1902, a cartoon had appeared in *The Washington Post* showing President Theodore Roosevelt on a hunting trip in Mississippi, refusing to shoot a small bear cub. A Brooklyn grocer, Mr Mitchom, showed the cartoon to his wife who sometimes made soft toys as a side line to sell in their shop. Mrs Mitchom made a toy bear cub and displayed it in the shop window together with the cartoon. The toy was an immediate success and as Mrs Mitchom was kept busy making more and more toy bears to sell, Mr Mitchom, fired with entrepreneurial zeal, wrote to the President to ask if he would allow the toy to be marketed under the name 'Teddy's Bear'. The President gave his permission and in 1903 the teddy bear was launched.

Unfortunately for Mr Mitchom, although he set up a company to manufacture the bears in a big way, he could not patent the name and it was not long before other toy makers all over America realized the potential of this new cuddly plaything. It was, in fact, an American who discovered 'Friend Petz' on the Steiff stall at the Leipzig Toy Fair in 1903 and immediately placed an order for three thousand. From that day on the name of Steiff has been synonymous all over the world with that of the teddy bear.

Britain also played an important role in the teddy bear's early history as it was the British firm of J. K. Farnell, established in 1840, that pioneered the development of a soft, plush mohair. The new fabric was ideally suited to the manufacture of furry toys and it was, in fact, this Yorkshire plush that Margarete Steiff used when making 'Friend Petz'. It was not long before the firm of Farnell was producing its own bears and even exporting them to Germany; one of the most famous bears of all, Winnie-the-Pooh, bought in Harrods in 1920, was a Farnell bear.

Winnie-the-Pooh, like many other early English bears, started life as Edward; I even know a seventy-seven-year-old French bear known as Edouard. These bears all seem to have been named after Edward VII who was also known as Teddy. Many people therefore claim that this is the origin of the name teddy bear. To complicate the story even more it is said that in 1880 Edward VII took a fancy to a small koala bear that had just arrived at London Zoo and that koala bears became known as teddy bears from then on!

Whatever the true origins of the first teddy bear, I feel that by some kind of evolutionary process he would have arrived on the scene sooner or later and whether he is called Teddy, Bruin, Petz, Edward, Rupert or Paddington does not really matter; his incredible staying power is proof of how much he has come to mean to so many.

There was an Old Person of Ware
    Who rode on the back of a Bear,
    When they ask'd, 'Does it trot?' –
    He said, 'Certainly not!
He's a Moppsikon Floppsikon Bear!'

EDWARD LEAR

The Teddy Bears

By Clara Andrews Williams

 *This book appeared in 1909 with delightful illustrations of teddy bears dressed in a wonderful array of Edwardian clothes. The story begins on the morning of Betty's eighth birthday.*

A t almost the first peep of the bright, warm, sunny day Betty awakened. 'Hurrah, I'm eight. Jack, wake up,' she cried. Jack sprang out of bed. They were dressed in a twinkle of the sun's eye, then together they ran to bid good-morning to father and mother. Early as it was, Mr and Mrs Gardener had risen before them and already were awaiting their children. Then eight kisses from each began really and truly the jolliest birthday for Betty.

Mother handed her a little note written on the funniest and tiniest sheet of paper with a picture of the cutest little tiny bear up at the top and Betty read slowly but eagerly –

'Join us in the garden, Betty, dear,
By the side of the high brick wall;
For until you and Jack come to play with us,
We are not happy at all.
With love and greetings for a happy birthday,
    The Teddy Bears.'

10

Betty folded the note carefully, and tenderly laid it in the drawer of her desk. 'I'll read it again after,' she said, 'but now let's hurry out and see.' So they rushed down, and what a wonderful party awaited them in the garden! Close to the high wall, sure enough, there sat a host of Teddy Bears. There were white ones and brown ones, large ones, small ones and medium ones, but one and all when they saw Betty coming, jumped up and ran to meet her. Betty was down on her knees in a minute. She really did not know which to hug and kiss first so she opened her arms wide and let them all cuddle in her lap and gave them a generous squeeze all together. 'Now I must give you each a name,' she said.

'Though we might name them after the people who gave them to you,' said Jack, 'because you know that mother and father and me and both grandpas and aunts and uncles, all gave them together.'

'Well! We never could have guessed this surprise if we'd thought and thought a whole year,' laughed Betty. 'But, Jack, if we name them Uncle Martin and Uncle Sky then it will be so mixy up when Uncle Martin and all really do come to play with us,' she objected.

'Tom Thumb! That's right, Betty, I did not think of that – '

'I'll call that big, biggest one "Plushkin" anyway because he's so very, very funny and warm like Grandma Picton's big, plush-covered easy chair. The rest will get names as we think of them in our play.'

And so they did. Betty and Jack and the bears shared many adventures, in the garden, at school, at the seaside, at Hallowe'en, the circus, winter sports and Christmas and the bears gradually acquired names: Racy, Climbus, Greedy Brown, Smallest, Clumsy, Della-kate, Plush-clever, Snow-white, and finally Plushkin's twin who turned up

under the Christmas tree wearing a Russian hat and tunic and announced:

'Oh, I am the twin of the white Plush-skin
And this I'll have you note,
Though I'm big as he, our shades don't agree;
So call me Brown Plush-Coat.'

Me and My Teddy Bear

By Jack Winters

Me and my Teddy Bear
Have no worries,
Have no care!
Me and my Teddy Bear
Just play and play all day.
I love my Teddy Bear,
He's got one eye and got no hair,
But I love my Teddy Bear,
We play and play all day!
Every night he's with me
When I climb up the stairs,
And by my bed he listens
      until I say my prayers!
Oh! Me and my Teddy Bear
Have no worries,
Have no care!
Me and my Teddy Bear
Just play and play all day.

Billy Bluegum

By Edward Dyson

'Billy Bluegum' first appeared as a serial in the Australian periodical 'The Bulletin' between 1904 and 1908 and tells how Billy Bluegum, an energetic koala bear raised in the comfort of the city, is inspired with a mission to go out and preach civilization to the bears of the bush. The illustrations were by Norman Lindsay.

Billy Bluegum never understood what power it was that moved him one still night in early Spring.

He went quietly to work, packed his gripsack and suit-case, put on his best frock-coat and his polished Paris hat and stole from the house.

That house had been his home ever since he was a 'Joey' or baby bear, a mere wisp of pale grey fluff without market value or table manners of any sort.

No bear ever had a better home or nicer people. His family were always kind to him. They were most considerate about treading on his toes, for instance. They rarely dropped candle fat in his hair, or rubbed treacle in his whiskers. His people built him a Queen Anne Villa in the nursery, dressed him becomingly, and taught him to eat peas with a fork. His feelings were often considered. They begged his pardon repeatedly. They even permitted him to wear an eyeglass.

Billy owed it to these good creatures that he was a most genteel bear, a bear who had enjoyed the advantages of civilization, and had kept silkworms; yet he was running away.

'It is ungrateful, this stealing from the house,' said Billy Bluegum in the long garden. 'It is ungrateful, and I fancy it is burglary. Yes, stealing from the house is burglary, but I hope it isn't bad form.'

13

Presently, he brightened up. 'After all, one can always apologise.' He took off his hat and bowed very politely to his old home. 'I beg yours,' said he.

After that he felt better. He pushed his luggage through the loose palings and went jauntily out into the vastness of over-the-way.

Billy's suit-case was marked 'W. Bluegum, Esq.' but his bag bore the name of a total stranger, one 'Public Loans', and had been the property of a Great Man, the chief parent of Billy's Boy. Billy was owned by the Boy and the Boy was owned by the Great Man.

The parent of Billy Bluegum's Boy was for many years a notorious statesman carrying on an extensive business all over Australia, during the whole of which time he had never been seen without the bag firmly grasped in his left hand. To it he resorted in all his difficulties. It had been the secret of his every success, and had saved the country nine times. . .

However, after a long career as a notorious statesman, the Great Man reformed and accepted a position of emolument under the Crown. Then the bag descended to Billy Bluegum with the Paris hats and a bobtailed shaving brush.

That there was a sort of magic in the bag no genteel reader of these surprising chronicles will deny. Billy took it with him because it balanced the suit-case so nicely.

'It is diplomatic to preserve one's balance,' said Billy Bluegum. 'There is a shocking lack of equipoise about a traveller with one bag.'

Billy prided himself on being a bear of the world, but in truth he knew nothing of far places beyond the busy town. If anyone had asked him why he was going he would have answered, 'Because,' which, as everybody knows who knows anything, explains everything.

Feelings in the air, faint scents, little longings, an inward force – all these things drove him out and on.

Billy had not time to wonder where he was going; he was too eager to get there. He was an extremely busy, native bear in a bell-topper hat, with an umbrella and much luggage, walking with quick, baby footsteps, like a feverish little elderly gentleman who is absolutely certain he will miss his train.

A short, stout, middle-aged bear dashing off at midnight, in possession of property that might be reasonably supposed to have been stolen, would certainly create scandal were he seen; but Billy had the road to himself. He passed unnoticed.

In 1918 Norman Lindsay produced his own children's book, 'The Magic Pudding', in which a close relative of Billy's appears by the name of Bunyip Bluegum.

Bunyip Bluegum's Reflections

By Norman Lindsay

I've got a stick to walk with.
I've got a mind to think with.
I've got a voice to talk with.
I've got an eye to wink with.
I've lots of teeth to eat with,
A brand new hat to bow with,
A pair of fists to beat with,
A rage to have a row with.
No joy it brings
    To have indeed
A lot of things
    One does not need.
Observe my doleful plight,
    For here am I without a crumb
    To satisfy a raging tum –
O what an oversight!

Tim Tubby Toes

By Harry Golding

 *First published in 1913 in the Ward Lock 'Little Wonder Series'.
My daughter has inherited a very small bear of the same date
and name who is definitely not allowed into the kitchen.*

Y ou like treacle, don't you? So did Tim. Perhaps you like it very much? You couldn't possibly like it more than Tim did.

The Grocer's boy must have dropped the jar when he went through the wood. First Tim smelt it, then he licked the outside, then he got the top off, and then – nasty Mr Lion came.

When it was safe to return, the jar had gone. Poor Tim, he had only such a tiny taste! But now he had what is called 'treacle on the brain'. It is a dreadful thing to have the matter with you.

'Poor dear,' said Mother Tubby Toes, 'he's getting very thin.' But wise old Father Tubby Toes only smoked his pipe, and said that treacle was bad for little bears.

At last Tim did the bravest thing he could have done. He went right up to Mr Lion and asked if he could have the jar back.

'The jar?' said Mr Lion. 'What for?'

'Just to lick,' said Tim timidly. It wasn't much to ask but the Lion grew quite angry and bared his ears.

Tim was still crying when the Spotted Panther came along. He hated the Lion like anything.

Tim is advised by the Spotted Panther to go to Human Town to find some more treacle which he does in plenty and discovers that too much treacle is far worse than none at all! He soon finds he has treacle inside him and treacle all over him and when he falls asleep his dreams are more treacly than ever. While he is asleep he is caught by the grocer and arrested but after some further sticky adventures he is eventually

16

rescued by the Spotted Panther who sees him safely home again.

The Spotted Panther suddenly popped up from nowhere. With his right paw he clutched at Tim and then turned and faced the crowd.

The crowd had never seen the Spotted Panther before and they did not wish to see him again. But he was really quite a kind-hearted creature and first took Timmy home as carefully as any nurse.

'Dear me, dear me!' said Mother Tubby Toes, when they arrived. Then she quickly undressed her little boy and plumped him into a bath as hot as he could bear. Afterwards there was a dose of nasty medicine to take. Tim was sure the spoon had never been so big before.

'Goodnight, dearie,' said Mother. 'I don't think you'll want to dream of treacle tonight.'

'Treacle's the horridest stuff that ever was,' said Tim.

But it isn't really – unless you take too much of it.

Teddy Bear cannot be seen
Until his face is nice and clean.
My Teddy nearly always cries
Because the soap goes in his eyes.

Rhyme from an early postcard

17

Edward

By Mrs H. C. Cradock

 *Mrs Cradock, better known for her Josephine books with their lovely illustrations by Honor Appleton, wrote several other teddy bear stories between the years 1915 to 1939.*

H e is a Teddy Bear, and quite lovely. He really is much lovelier than other Teddy Bears – quite a special sort of one. If you ask *how* he is different, and why I say he is so nice, I don't quite know how to answer; I can only say if you lived with him as we do – Tony and I – you would know without being told; directly you looked at him you would know.

He is only eight inches tall from the top of his head to the bottom of his – I was going to say *feet*; but he hasn't any feet. He is one of the hollow, soft kinds of Teddies, with a head and arms, and the rest of him is a sort of skirt. You can put your hands inside him, and make him bow and clap his hands, and things like that. His eyes are really the large, round heads of two pins; but they look *just* like eyes. His nose is black silk threads.

I don't know how he manages to change the look on his face; but he does. He can look sad or merry. When he cries he just puts up both hands and covers his eyes, and then you always want to hug him again. His cheeks are getting rather bare with all the hugging he gets.

Mummy says he is a very special kind of person. She says, 'There are bears *and* bears.' That means some are nice and some are not. At least I think it means that, or something like that. It is rather hard sometimes to understand what grown-ups mean. When Mummy said that, Tony stared but said nothing. Tony has very blue eyes, and he stares solemnly at people without speaking, and then when they are gone he says, 'What is bears *and* bears?' and I tell him. He is five and I am eight.

Even Daddy says, when he is speaking about Teddy, 'Yes, he

18

is a fine chap.' Nanny won't let *me* say 'chap'; she says it's vulgar, so I said, 'Daddy says, "Teddy's a fine chap,"' and she said, 'That's different,' and I said, 'Why?' and she said, 'You're not a man, are you?'

One afternoon Teddy had to go to a very important meeting. He told us he was Prime Minister now, and could make any laws he liked, and everybody would have to do what he said. 'If I made a law that no ladies were to have golden evening frocks they wouldn't *have* to,' he said.

Poor Mrs Edward turned pale, and a tear trickled down her cheek.

'I didn't say I *should* make a law like that,' said Teddy. 'But I could if I liked. Fear not, Louisa.'

Mrs Edward cheered up.

Teddy set off for Parliament with his walking-stick, and a flower in his button-hole. You could tell he was Prime Minister; he looked so important. He wouldn't let anybody go with him. He just waved us off when we tried to follow him. By the time he reached the Parliament House he looked more than ever like a Prime Minister – *so* important. He called out that he would tell us all about it when he came home for tea.

We were anxious all the afternoon, wondering what laws he would make. Daddy said it was an eventful day for the country.

Well, we had just sat down to tea when in he walked, with a grand air and quite calm.

I took his stick, and Tony his coat, and Mrs Edward pushed his chair nearer the table for him. We had to be careful with the Prime Minister.

At tea, grand as he was, he was very kind; and when we asked him who was at the Parliament, he said, 'Nobody – only me.'

'Did you make any new laws?' I asked.

'Yes,' he said, 'I made these:

1. Nobody need eat rice pudding any more.
2. Nobody must be left out in the dark
    after picnics.
3. People can go to bed just when they like.
4. People can put elbows on the table if they like.
5. Nobody need eat fat.
6. People can have as much pocket-money as they like.
7. It does not matter at all if you forget to say "please" and
    "thank you".
8. People can make as many crumbs on the floor as they
    like.
9. Nobody must let soap get into your eyes when they are
    washing you.
10. Nobody need go into the drawing room if they don't want
    to when callers come.'

'Oh, Teddy dear, what lovely laws! You are an unselfish boy –
Prime Minister, I mean. There is only one law about you and Mrs
Edward, and all the others are about us.'

Daddy said the country would begin to sit up and go ahead
now.

After tea, when it was nearly bed-time, Teddy said he would
stop being Prime Minister now, because he wanted to sit on my knee
again and lean his head against me, and me to tell him a story
beginning, 'Once upon a time there was a little Teddy Bear.'

I really *couldn't* nurse a Prime Minister and tell him stories.

So Tony nursed Mrs Edward, and I nursed Teddy, and they were so cosy and comfy with their soft heads leaning against us and their faces turned up to look at us.

You can't wonder that I said there never was such a lovely Teddy in all the world, can you?

From *The Best Teddy Bear in the World*

Lullaby

Go to sleep my Teddy Bear.
Close your little button eyes,
And let me smooth your hair.
It feels so soft and silky that,
I'd love to cuddle down by you,
So,
Go to sleep, my darling Teddy Bear.

Anon

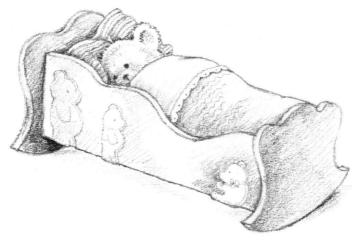

Leaky Ted

By Charles Headland

This piece is from a collection of unpublished stories called 'Here We Are', describing a little girl's toys. They were written in India in the late '20s for a much- loved and sadly missed only child while she was back in England at school. The original manuscript is beautifully bound in hand- tooled leather and the stories are all illustrated with portraits of the toys.

When you came to live with our baby, Leaky Ted, we thought you were the most beautiful Teddy we had ever seen. In your gay, blue frock and your pale pink neck ribbon you looked such a cuddly pet for a little girl. And how she loved you! How we all loved you! How gaily you used to chase the tears away when you pranced for us to the silly little tune of 'Teddy's little dancing song is Teedle, teedle, tee'.

Do you remember when you went to England, Leaky Ted? That was a big experience for a little bear your size. And after that followed many other adventures in that new land. Perhaps the one we minded most was when your little mother suddenly realized you had turned from a pretty white Ted to a dingy gray one and that all your chubby life was oozing away through the big holes in your skin. Poor Ted! You had to have your one and only bath in LUX and were hung by a string to the clothes line to dry. We didn't like seeing you hang there, old Ted, and we were *so* glad when you could come down. After that you were nicely mended, with all your leaks stopped and you had on a brave new frock.

Fuzzy Wuzzy

Fuzzy Wuzzy was a bear
a bear was Fuzzy Wuzzy.
When Fuzzy Wuzzy lost his hair
he wasn't fuzzy, was he?

Traditional

The Great Lavender Bear

By Frank L. Baum

 *This is a chapter from one of the many 'Oz' books, 'The Lost Princess of Oz', written in 1917. It tells the story of how Princess Ozma suddenly disappears and search parties are sent out to try to find her. One of these involves Cayke, the Cookie Cook, and the Frogman.*

It was a pleasant place to wander in and the two travellers were proceeding at a brisk pace when suddenly a voice shouted: 'Halt!'

They looked around in surprise, seeing at first no one at all. Then from behind a tree there stepped a brown, fuzzy bear, whose head came about as high as Cayke's waist – and Cayke was a small woman. The bear was chubby as well as fuzzy; his body was even puffy, while his legs and arms seemed jointed at the knees and elbows and fastened to his body by pins or rivets. His ears were round in shape and stuck out in a comical way, while his round, black eyes were bright and sparkling as beads. Over his shoulder the little brown bear bore a gun with a tin barrel. The barrel had a cork in the end of it and a string was attached to the cork and to the handle of the gun.

Both the Frogman and Cayke gazed hard at this curious bear, standing silent for some time. But finally the Frogman recovered from his surprise and remarked:

23

his surprise and remarked:

'It seems to me that you are stuffed with sawdust and ought not to be alive.'

'That's all you know about it,' answered the little Brown Bear in a squeaky voice. 'I am stuffed with a very good quality of curled hair and my skin is the best plush that was ever made. As for my being alive, that is my own affair and cannot concern you at all – except that it gives me the privilege to say you are my prisoners.'

'Prisoners! Why do you speak such nonsense?' asked the Frogman angrily. 'Do you think we are afraid of a toy bear with a toy gun?'

'You ought to be,' said the confident reply, 'for I am merely the sentry guarding the way to Bear Centre, which is a city containing hundreds of my race who are ruled by a very powerful sorcerer known as the Lavender Bear. He ought to be a purple colour, you know, seeing he is a King; but he's only light lavender, which is, of course, second-cousin to royal purple. So, unless you come with me peaceably, as my prisoners, I shall fire my gun and bring a hundred bears – of all sizes and colours – to capture you.'

'Why do you wish to capture us?' inquired the Frogman, who had listened to this speech with much astonishment.

'I don't wish to, as a matter of fact,' replied the little Brown Bear, 'but it is my duty to, because you are now trespassing on the domain of His Majesty the King of Bear Centre. Also I will admit that things are rather quiet in our city, just now, and the excitement of your capture, followed by your trial and execution, should afford us much entertainment.'

'We defy you!' said the Frogman.

'Oh, no; don't do that,' pleaded Cayke, speaking to her companion. 'He says his King is a scorcerer, so perhaps it is he or one of his bears who ventured to steal my jewelled dishpan. Let us go to the City of the Bears and discover if my dishpan is there.'

'I must now register one more charge against you,' remarked the little Brown Bear, with evident satisfaction. 'You have just accused us of stealing, and that is such a dreadful thing to say that I am quite sure our noble King will command you to be executed.'

'But how could you execute us?' inquired the Cookie Cook.

'I've no idea. But our King is a wonderful inventor and there is no doubt he can find a proper way to destroy you. So, tell me, are you going to struggle, or will you go peaceably to meet your doom?'

It was all so ridiculous that Cayke laughed aloud and even the Frogman's wide mouth curled in a smile. Neither was a bit afraid to go to the Bear City so the Frogman said: 'Lead the way, little Bear, and we will follow without a struggle.'

'That's very sensible of you; very sensible, indeed!' declared the Brown Bear. 'So – for-ward *march!*' and with the command he turned around and began to waddle along a path that led between the trees.

Cayke and the Frogman, as they followed their conductor, could scarce forbear laughing at his stiff, awkward manner of walking and, although he moved his stuffy legs fast, his steps were so short that they had to go slowly in order not to run into him. But after a time they reached a large, circular space in the centre of the forest, which was clear of any stumps or underbrush. The ground was covered by a soft, gray moss, pleasant to tread upon. All the trees surrounding this space seemed to be hollow and had round holes in their trunks, set a little way above the ground, but otherwise there was nothing unusual about the place and nothing, in the opinion of the prisoners, to indicate a settlement. But the little Brown Bear said in a proud and impressive voice (although it still squeaked):

'This is the wonderful city known to fame as Bear Centre!'

'But there are no houses; there are no bears living here at all!' exclaimed Cayke.

'Oh indeed!' retorted their captor and raising his gun he pulled the trigger. The cork flew out of the tin barrel with a loud 'pop!' and at once from every hole in every tree within view of the clearing appeared the head of a bear. They were so many colours and of many sizes, but all were made in the same manner as the bear who had met and captured them.

At first a chorus of growls arose and then a sharp voice cried:
'What has happened, Corporal Waddle?'

'Captives, Your Majesty!' answered the Brown Bear. 'Intruders upon our domain and slanderers of our good name.'

'Ah, that's important,' answered the voice.

Then from out of the hollow trees tumbled a whole regiment of stuffed bears, some carrying tin swords, some popguns and others long spears with gay ribbons tied to the handles. There were hundreds of them, altogether, and they quickly formed a circle around the Frogman and the Cookie Cook but kept at a distance and left a large space for the prisoners to stand in.

Presently, this circle parted and into the centre of it stalked a huge toy bear of a lovely lavender colour. He walked upon his hind legs, as did all the others, and on his head he wore a tin crown set with diamonds and amethysts, while in one paw he carried a short wand of some glittering metal that resembled silver but wasn't.

'His Majesty the King!' shouted Corporal Waddle, and all the bears bowed low. Some bowed so low that they lost their balance and toppled over, but they soon scrambled up again and the Lavender King squatted on his haunches before the prisoners and gazed at them steadily with his bright pink eyes.

The Teddy Bear Scouts

By Jessie Pope

 This extract is from a tiny, teddy bear-sized book published by Blackie in 1915.

The Teddy Bear Patrol you here observe,
Renowned for courage, nimbleness and nerve.
Three Teddy scouts, each peeping from his tent
One night said, 'Let's go hunting!' and they went.

They had a famous breakfast for a start.
Their names were Blisters, Bullyrag and Bart.
But as they crossed the sea Bart was upset;
He really got uncomfortably wet.

Still, he could swim, so with a cheery smile
He sat at safety on a desert isle,
Until some savages, all painted red,
Bound him with ropes and hit him on the head.

But Bullyrag and Blisters set him free,
Approaching cautiously from tree to tree.
And so once more they sally out to hunt,
Blisters behind and Bullyrag in front.

But first across the yellow sands they trip,
With towels round their shoulders for a dip;
Bart stalks a tiger-cat for half a day;
But when his prey looks round, Bart walks away.

Blisters the better part of valour showed,
In hastily retiring from a toad.
While Bullyrag, not looking where he goes,
Falls in a pit and wildly waves his toes.

The others gently lift him from the hole,
And make him have a nap upon a pole.
But soon he's well, and then, with merry shouts
They dance the war dance of the Teddy Scouts.

The Little Brown Bears

By Christine Temple

Stories about the Little Brown Bears first appeared in 'Little Dots Annual', published by the Religious Tract Society during the 1920s and '30s.

Once upon a time there was a family of little brown bears, and they all lived together in a tiny house with a red roof.

There were so many of them that their Mummie could not remember all their names. These were Marmeduke, Clarence and Cuthbert, Archibald, Frederick, Algernon and Wee One. Mummie Bear always remembered *his* name, partly because he was the smallest and partly because he was so naughty; all the little brown bears were naughty, but Wee One was the naughtiest.

RAT-TAT! went the postman's knock one morning, when the little brown bears were sitting round the breakfast table eating their porridge.

They put down their spoons and rushed to the front door to pick up the letter.

'It's an invitation to a party!' said Mummie Bear, putting on her spectacles, 'from Mrs Brown-toes, for next Tuesday afternoon!'

The little bears were very excited! They could hardly wait, but Tuesday came at last.

'Now you must promise to be good,' said Mummie Bear as she brushed their fur. 'Don't lose your pocket hankies and don't lick your paws when you've finished your tea!'

'We'll be good, Mummie,' promised the little bears, as they hurried off.

It was a lovely party! There were a lot of other little brown bears. First they played games and then they had tea. But in the middle of tea, when no one was looking, Wee One took up a bun and threw it across the table, and it hit Algernon on the nose.

'Who did that?' Algernon asked in a surprised tone.

Then all the little bears stared at Wee One.

They stared hard! What do you think had happened?

Wee One was licking the crumbs off his plate!

Then he climbed on the table, before anyone could stop him, and stood on his head in the middle of a pink raspberry jelly! He was the naughtiest little bear at the party and his brothers were very cross with him!

When the little bears saw Wee One climb on the table and stand on his head in the middle of the pink raspberry jelly, they all scrambled up on their chairs and tried to catch him.

They climbed onto the table, and some of them put their feet into the custard by mistake, and some of them tripped over the blancmange, and some of them fell into the fruit salad, but they couldn't catch Wee One.

Down he jumped, and ran round and round the room.

And all the little bears raced after him!

But Marmeduke caught him at last, and, holding him firmly by the ear, marched him up to Mrs Brown-toes.

'Please, he'll have to go home!' said Marmeduke. 'He's been very naughty!'

But Mrs Brown-toes would not hear of it.

There were crackers and balloons and all sorts of surprises for the little bears.

And when seven o'clock struck, they gathered up their toys, and said 'good-bye' to Mrs Brown-toes; and after thanking her most politely for the party, they all ran home again.

'And were you good?' asked Mummie Bear, when she had heard all about the party.

'I wasn't very good, Mummie,' said Wee One sleepily. 'I threw a bun at Algernon, and I. . .' he paused for a minute and then went on more sleepily than ever, 'I licked my paws after tea . . . and I licked my plate, and I licked. . .' But in the middle of telling his Mummie how naughty he had been, Wee One fell fast asleep.

Teddy Brown

By Ida Bohatta

I know my numbers up to four
And my letters up to Y.
I'm certain that I'll learn no more,
How ever hard I try.
My mother says I now must learn
To puff and pant and growl,
Like proper grown-up bears all do
When they are on the prowl.

From *The Brown Family*, translated
from the German by June Heard

31

Pooh

By Christopher Milne

 *In his sensitive autobiography 'The Enchanted Places', Christopher Milne depicts his childhood world with a touching realism that counteracts much of the whimsy of his father's books. In this extract he introduces us to Pooh.*

Pooh was only a year younger than I was, and my inseparable companion. As you find us in the poem 'Us Two', so we were in real life. Every child has his favourite toy, and every only child has a special need for one. Pooh was mine, and probably, clasped in my arms, not really very different from the countless other bears clasped in the arms of countless other children. From time to time he went to the cleaners, and from time to time ears had to be sewn on again, lost eyes replaced and paws renewed.

The bear took his place in the nursery and gradually he began to come to life. It started in the nursery; it started with me.

It could really start nowhere else, for the toys lived in the nursery and they were mine and I played with them. And as I played with them and talked to them and gave them voices to answer with, so they began to breathe. But alone I couldn't take them very far. I needed help. So my mother joined me and she and I and the toys played together, and gradually more life, more character flowed into them, until they reached a point at which my father could take over. Then, as the first stories were written, the cycle was repeated. The Pooh in my arms, the Pooh sitting opposite me at the breakfast table, was a Pooh who had climbed trees in search of honey, who had got stuck in a rabbit hole, who was 'a bear of no brain at all'. . .

A hand-made Pooh bear that sat on A. A. Milne's desk until his death in 1956 when it was given to a charity sale. It is now in a private collection.

Col. Bob Henderson's 'Teddy Girl', a 1903 Steiff bear in beautiful condition.
Early bears such as this are now much sought-after and fetch record prices at Sothebys.
It was also a 1906 Steiff bear, called 'Growler', that E. H. Shepard used as his model
for Winnie-the-Pooh.

The Auction at Pooh Corner

By E. S. Turner (after A. A. Milne)

 *The following piece appeared in Punch on 14th February 1968, after an original E. H. Shepard drawing had sold at Sothebys for a record £1,200. It had previously belonged to Prince Pudukota of Madras.*

Pooh was humming a good hum, such as is hummed boastfully to others.

> 'Sotheby, Botheby,
> Tiddely-Pom!
> The sketch of our picnic
> Has sold for a bomb.'

'He means twelve hundred pounds,' explained Piglet.

'That's peanuts,' said Eeyore.

At the mention of peanuts they all blinked and were silent for a minute. Then Pooh recovered his spirits and said:

'I shouldn't be surprised if we all finished up at the Tate.'

'We would have been there already,' said Eeyore, 'if you had learnt to say Wham and Pow and Aaaaaargh.'

'Anyway,' said Piglet, 'our pictures fetch as much as some old paperweights I could mention and some important sixteenth-century Arabian manuscripts I won't mention.'

'Here's Christopher Robin, who has been having Education all morning,' said Pooh. 'He has lots of brain.'

Christopher Robin began telling them about things like Shifting Trends and Underlying Social Significance and What the Market Will Bear and the Challenge to Pop Art of Nursery Trade.

Piglet soon excused himself and went off to pick daisies.

'You could all have been famous already,' said Christopher

Robin, 'if you had not been famous all the time. I suppose it's my fault really.'

Pooh began another hum.

> 'Ho-tiddely-ho!
> We haven't a chance,
> We haven't got So-
> cial Significance.'

'There's one thing you haven't told us,' complained Eeyore. 'Who gets the twelve hundred pounds?'

'The Prince of Pudukota, of course,' said Pooh.

'There you go. You're making things up again,' grumbled Eeyore. Nobody could persuade him that there was a real Prince of Pudukota, who once had an English nanny, and rose to become a client of Sotheby's.

'Why,' asked Eeyore, 'does a man who doesn't exist get twelve hundred pounds for a picture he hasn't drawn?'

Christopher Robin said that Art was like that.

Meanwhile, Pooh was sprawling on the ground, making the face-you-make-when-a-hum-gets-stuck, so they left him muttering to himself.

> 'Isn't it rum
> When a hum won't come?
> I ought to be rich – so there!
> Isn't it funny how a bear makes money,
> But none of it sticks to the bear?'

The Vain Teddy

By Rose Fyleman

 *Rose Fyleman was the first person to encourage A. A. Milne to write for children and it was she who published some of his verses before they appeared as the collection 'When We Were Very Young' in 1924.*

There was once a toy Teddy-bear who belonged to a little girl called Peggy. He was very big, almost as big as Peggy herself, and I am sorry to say that he was very vain.

You see, people always said, when they saw him, 'What a beautiful Teddy-bear!'

Peggy thought there was no one like him in the world. He always wore a blue bow, and she even made a blue silk cap for him, which he wore on the top of his head. It really made him look rather ridiculous, but it had a feather in it, and the vain Teddy thought it suited him beautifully, though he would have preferred pink.

'Pink is really my colour,' he said to himself. 'I wish Peggy would realize how well I should look in pink.'

He grew more and more conceited every day. The other toys didn't like him at all. He used to sit in the corner and never join in their talk. If anyone spoke to him, he just said 'Yes' or 'No' in a proud voice, and stared at the ceiling.

But he was punished in the end.

One day Peggy's mother bought a packet of pink dye for Peggy's Sunday frock (which had faded very badly in the sun), mixed it in a great big pot, and left it standing on the kitchen table.

The Teddy-bear was sitting on the window-sill just over the table.

'How pretty that dye is!' he thought. 'What a lovely colour! If only my cap were that colour, how handsome I should look!'

Then he had an idea. 'If I lean over,' he thought, 'my cap will drop in, and then it will get dyed.'

He leaned over.

'Mind! Mind!' sang the canary.

But he took no notice. He leaned over farther and farther. Suddenly – splash! splash! He had fallen right into the pot of dye!

You never saw such a comical sight as he was when they got him out. Pink all over! Peggy still loved him as much as ever, but his appearance was utterly spoiled.

'What a funny Teddy!' people said now. In time he got used to it, but he never really got over it. He was never known to squeak again.

These jolly little Teddy Bears,
Who always love to play,
When hugged by little boys and girls,
They'll scare all gloom away.

Anon

From an advertisement, 1923

Bibble, Bobble and Bubble

By Josephine Hatcher

This extract from a small book, published in the '40s, was written and illustrated by a child of seven. Of course, the unfortunate Bubble is the victor in the end.

Bobble was a fat, lazy bear,
Bibble was a thin, mean bear,
Bubble was a little, kind bear.
Bobble wore smart red trousers
Kept up by a red belt,
Bibble wore smart black trousers
Kept up by a black belt
And Bubble wore old blue trousers
Kept up by old black braces.
Bobble had a rich Aunt, who sent him
money every Tuesday
But nobody ever sent Bubble a letter.
Bobble lived in a big, fat house,
Bibble lived in a tall, thin house
And Bubble lived in a small, ordinary house.
Bobble had 40 jars of honey in his big cupboard,
Bibble had 39 jars of honey in his tall cupboard
And Bubble had 7 jars of honey in his little cupboard.
Bobble did not look after his garden.
Bibble did not look after his garden.
But Bubble grew lovely flowers in his garden.
Bobble had Bibble for a friend.
Bibble had Bobble for a friend.
But Bubble had no friend.

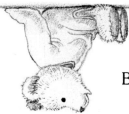

Night Bears

By Wilma Horsbrugh

Three little bears
From nowhere in particular,
    nowhere in particular,
    nowhere at all,
Came up the stairs
And climbed the perpendicular,
    climbed the perpendicular,
    nursery wall.

They sat upon the ceiling
And sang with all their might
Songs so full of feeling
They lasted half the night.

A funny thing it seemed
For little bears to do.
I think I must have dreamed
Those little bears, don't you?

For when the songs were ended
Then down the walls they slid,
And when they had descended
Do you know what they did?

Those three little bears
Went nowhere in particular,
    nowhere in particular,
    flat or perpendicular.
    nowhere at all.

Tidgie's Innings

By V. H. Drummond

 *This story, written in 1947, begins in the toy department of a large London store where two toy cricket teams are displayed for sale. One team, the Wouffle Ramblers, who are eleven velvet dogs, challenge the other team, the E-Zonga-Bee, eleven velour teddy bears, to a match in Kensington Gardens at midnight on the first full moon in June. They all agree to come from the houses of the families to whom they have been sold, the Muscovy Duck offering to act as a taxi to make sure they all manage to get there. Tidgie, the smallest of the teddy bears, is eventually sold and given as a present to a little girl called Sarah who completely ignores him. The night comes for the great match and the Muscovy Duck escorts all the competitors, including the reluctant Tidgie, to Kensington Gardens. We join the story at the climax of the match which started at midnight and has continued into the following morning.*

T hen the people who walk in the Park and the children and nurses came. They all stared with amazement at the cricket match.

'Look!' they cried, clustering forward. 'Some toy bears and some toy dogs playing cricket. This is a strange sight to see!'

But the cricketers went on in spite of them all.

At last the bears had batted and there was only Tidgie left to go in.

'We have twenty-four more runs to make to beat them,' said Philip Watson [the captain of the bears' team]. 'Tidgie is the worst bear in the team. He could never make twenty-four runs. He will get caught out or bowled out straight away!' Poor Philip Watson was in despair.

Tidgie walked to the wicket with his bat in his paw; he hated cricket, but he hated this moment more than any other.

41

'I know I shall be out first ball,' he sighed. 'I wish I could make twenty-four runs to save the Zonga-Bee!'

But he shivered and shook with fright, and his poor little furry knees trembled. He glanced nervously at the crowd, and there to his surprise and joy he saw Sarah standing right in the front row. She smiled at him in a very encouraging way. . . At once Tidgie's fright left him and his furry knees ceased to tremble.

When he knew that Sarah was watching him he felt as brave as a lion. 'As long as I stare at the ball I know I shall hit it,' he said to himself, whereupon he hit a mighty swipe in a kind of backwards swerve that went over Mr Green's lodge and hit a policeman on the helmet in the Bayswater Road. The policeman graciously fielded the ball and the crowd clapped loudly.

Next Tidgie made a fine shot which landed in the chimney of Mr Green's lodge. Mr Green kindly climbed onto the roof and fielded it. 'Hurrah! Hurrah!' everyone shouted.

Between each of these magnificent hits Tidgie bowed to Sarah and grinned at her.

His next ball went into the flower bed and the Wouffle fielder had to climb the palings and crawl carefully amongst the flowers to find it.

Sarah smiled and clapped her hands. 'Clever bear!' she cried. Tidgie's last and most amazing shot went over the trees and was heard to splash into the Serpentine. One of the Wouffle fielders had to take off his flannel shirt and dive in after the ball, which he could not find in spite of splashing and growling about in the water . . . but nobody cared, for Tidgie had hit four boundaries and the E-Zonga-Bee had won the match!

Philip Watson and the rest of the team hurried up to Tidgie and patted him on the back and shook him by the paw.

'Well played, Tidgie! You have saved the E-Zonga-Bee!' they cried.

Then the dogs and the bears lined up in front of each other with the china pig in the middle and shouted: 'Three cheers!' And all the children scolded them for running away. But most of them were too pleased to have their toys back again to be really cross.

Sarah picked up Tidgie and kissed him. 'I am very proud of you,' she said as she carried him off.

All the crowd cheered, and Tidgie felt very happy.

For ever after Sarah took Tidgie with her wherever she went . . . right until she was quite a grown-up girl.

He rode with her in the pram to the park, he travelled to the seaside with her, and to the country to stay with her Granny. He always sat beside her at meals, and she even took him to parties.

Nannie often had to wash him, and much of the stuffing came out of his body, but he never played cricket again, and he was always, always happy.

Teddy be nimble,
Teddy be quick,
Teddy Jump over
The candle stick.

Traditional

The Jolly Bear

By Charlotte Hough

A lot of people do not care
For this extremely jolly bear.
They feel that they can do without
Being generally messed about.
He cheerfully upsets their games,
And calls them all peculiar names,
Like 'Fatty', 'Loony', 'Mange' or 'Bulky',
And then complains that they look sulky.
He says he'd like to see a few more
Good sports with a sense of humour.
'Come on!' he yells. 'Just follow me,
And we will have a jamboree!'
But just as soon as they've clapped eyes on
Him they're over the horizon.
They've gone because they've had enough
Of someone who is always rough.
Uninvited, large and hearty,
That bear turns up at every party.
And I really think he might
Not hug them all so very tight.
I'm sure it is not good for you
To constantly be black and blue.
It leaves you very short of breath
Being practically squeezed to death.
He's certainly the life and soul
When he punches Mildred Mole,
But it's hard to keep admiring
A tireless bear who is so tiring.
It's strange how it can irritate,
Just being too affectionate.

44

Stubbington Manor

By Lady Elizabeth Gorrell

 *An extract from one of 'The Bear Garden' books written between 1935 and 1945. A rich lady has bequeathed her wealth, which includes a stately home, to Stubbins, a small Koala Bear, who decides to take up residence with some of his friends.*

The sun shone brightly into the kitchen of Stubbington Manor. Breakfast was over and the post had come. Burnett, the Butler, had a letter from Mr Alexander, and he had just read it to Mrs Bathe, the cook, a round, rosy woman who had taken it from him and was rereading it out loud. Edith, the housemaid, was listening with pursed lips.

'Seven young gentlemen,' she said. 'Not quite what we've been used to; nice for my carpets too, I expect.'

Burnett too looked grave and even a little anxious. 'It seems James is to take the car up on Thursday in time to drive the gentlemen back here for tea – a bit of a squash; he had best take the Rolls, and even then it will be a close fit, I should say.'

'Well,' said Edith, 'Thursday is Thursday, and not very far away; I must be airing my linen. I suppose Mr Stubbins will have the Queen's Room and the other gentlemen must just sort themselves. A nice state my drawing room is likely to be with seven smoking and trampling all over it.'

Thursday morning came, a lovely sunshiny day. Stubbington Manor looked its best. The great magnolia which covered its front was in full flower. Inside the house, there were flowers everywhere, a wood fire burnt in the oak-panelled hall and one in the library arranged by Edith to look as inviting as possible. She had put out many ash-trays and removed the lovely Persian mat to the end of the room furthest from the fire-place.

45

The Queen's room, with its huge oak bed with four posts, another of those in which Queen Elizabeth had spent the night on one of her many journeys, was beautifully prepared for Mr Stubbins – not a crease on the coverlet with its dim-hued silks, its monograms and patterns. Edith moved about arranging things, now and then shaking her head and murmuring, 'Seven gentlemen!'

Mrs Bathe was warm and flustered, for several days she had been preparing what she thought the gentlemen would most like to eat – cakes full of plums, delicious rolls, cheese straws, and many other delicacies crowded the larder shelves, ready to tempt the new owner of the house.

'Lord Rushington anyhow will know what's what,' she thought as she spread out a row of juicy peaches. Privately she thought 'Stubbins' a common name, and when Lord Rushington was seen on the list her mind had been decidedly relieved.

And now the house was ready: everything was in apple-pie order, everything likely to please the gentlemen had been, as far as possible, provided for, and the hour had come. Burnett took up his post upon the wide, front-door steps, Mrs Bathe watched from the hall window, Edith hovered on the oak staircase. Suddenly there was a stir, the Butler turned round and signed excitedly to Mrs Bathe, who signed excitedly to Edith: the green Rolls was seen making its majestic progress up the long drive; it swept in a stately manner up to the front door and stopped.

James, the chauffeur, did not at once spring to open the door as they were accustomed to see him do when old Mrs Markes was in the car. Indeed, looking to see why he did not, Burnett thought instantly he must be ill: the chauffeur sat as if he was stuffed, his face scarlet, staring straight before him. Then with a jerk he moved, going round to the door of the car. He opened it and stood aside, holding it.

'The car is empty,' thought Burnett, peering forward. 'They haven't come,' thought Mrs Bathe, peeping through the window.

'What's up, James?' called Burnett, taking a step forward. James, his face still scarlet, stood stiffly at the door of the car and did not move.

Suddenly there was a stir and before the astonished eyes of Burnett and Mrs Bathe a small, a very small, figure descended in a bumbling jump and stood upon the steps below – a little brownish-grey Koala Bear, standing erect, looking curiously up at the house and the astonished Burnett.

Another movement and a large ginger-coloured Bear appeared. 'More like a big teddy,' thought Burnett, who was rooted to the spot. This Bear reached the side of the smaller one and together they bounced up the steps and stood at the Butler's feet. The  larger Bear spoke in a deep, rather loud voice. 'This is Mr Stubbins,' he said.

The Butler blinked, swallowed hard, shut his eyes a moment and then looked again: they were still there – not only that but other Bears were descending from the car, a lanky one of a much darker colour than the other two, wearing a fine pair of plum-coloured, velvet trousers, and one more like the first one, only he stuck out more in front and held his head very far back and wore a coat covered with buttons of all sorts and sizes. 'Crumbs,' muttered the dumbfounded Butler.

Stubbins, on being thus introduced, bowed very low and turning to Albert, said very simply, 'This is Albert.'

'Mr Bear!' hissed Albert in his ear. . .

Albert sighed heavily; he was tired with the excitement of the journey and all the anxiety of remembering how to make a good impression. But he pulled himself together and as each Bear bounced in his own peculiar way up the steps he introduced them to the Butler, who still seemed thunder-struck.

'Mr V. T. Trousers.' Velvet Trousers bowed. 'Mr S. Leepie.' Sleepie opened his eyes wider than usual and gave a friendly, sleepy little bow.

'Lord Rushington.' Here the Butler bowed; Lord Rushington passed him grandly, only raising a paw in acknowledgement. 'Mr G. S. Y. Rup,' went on Albert ceremoniously: the fat Bear smiled broadly and licked his lips to which clung a few remnants of the stick of barley-sugar which he had been sucking under the pretence that he felt sick in the car. . .

The Bears were introduced to Mrs Bathe and Edith, to whom they bowed gravely.

'Shall I show you your rooms, Sir, or would you care for some tea first?' asked Mrs Bathe, while Burnett went down the steps to superintend the unloading of the car of the many strange packages with which it was crammed.

'Tea first,' exclaimed Golden Syrup, pushing the last piece of barley-sugar into his mouth.

'Will you have tea or see the house, Stub?' asked Albert.

'Oh,' said Stubbins, turning pink, 'shall we have tea first?'

The chairs which had been set out round the long, narrow oak table which stood in the wide bay window, were used by the Bears only as places from which to climb onto the table, where they sat in a decorous ring round the food. Albert pointed out a badly tied parcel, which, when Edith, moving as if in a trance, unwrapped it, was found to contain some doll's cups and saucers and some even smaller doll's house ones, none of them very clean. Tea was poured into these and one set before each Bear. Albert said they would like to be left alone to have their tea, adding that they would ring when they had finished. Burnett showed them the electric bell-push on the table, and he, Mrs Bathe and Edith left the room; but they had not reached the kitchen, walking in silence and amazement, before a hard peal on the bell stopped them.

'One of them Bears has sat on the bell, as like as not,' said Mrs Bathe.

48

Burnett turned on his heel and solemnly paced down the passage again and back into the hall.

The Bears sat demurely in their places: every plate was empty.

Edward George St Clare

I'm really Edward George St Clare,
Aubrey Adolphus de la Bear
Son and Heir of the Baron Bear.
So please me, squeeze me, I don't care.

From an early autograph book

Aloysius

By Evelyn Waugh

 *Sebastian's bear in 'Brideshead Revisited' was inspired by Sir John Betjeman's bear, Archie, who accompanied him to Oxford in the '20s where he and Waugh were undergraduates together. In the television series of 'Brideshead Revisited' the part of Aloysius was played by Peter Bull's bear, Delicatessen.*

I knew Sebastian by sight long before I met him. That was unavoidable for, from his first week, he was the most conspicuous man of his year by reason of his beauty, which was arresting, and his eccentricities of behaviour, which seemed to know no bounds. My first sight of him was as we passed in the door of Germer's, and, on that occasion, I was struck less by his looks than by the fact that he was carrying a large teddy-bear.

'That,' said the barber, as I took his chair, 'was Lord Sebastian Flyte. A *most* amusing young gentleman.'

'Apparently,' I said coldly.

'The Marquis of Marchmain's second boy. His brother, the Earl of Brideshead, went down last term. Now he was *very* different, a very quiet gentleman, quite like an old man. What do you suppose Lord Sebastian wanted? A hair brush for his teddy-bear; it had to have very stiff bristles, *not*, Lord Sebastian said, to brush him with, but to threaten him with a spanking when he was sulky. He bought a very nice one with an ivory back and he's having 'Aloysius' engraved on it – that's the bear's name.' The man, who, in his time, had had ample chance to tire of undergraduate fantasy, was plainly captivated by him.

Eighty-year-old Delicatessen, so called because he was discovered languishing on the back shelf of a delicatessen store in a small town in America for sixty years. He was rescued and brought to England by the late Peter Bull.

The late Sir John Betjeman named his much-loved bear Archibald Ormsby-Gore after a favourite music-hall character. This drawing is from an early photograph and shows Archie in his youth.

Archie

By Sir John Betjeman

Safe were those evenings in the pre-war world
When firelight shone on green linoleum;
I heard the church bells hollowing out the sky,
Deep beyond deep, like never ending stars,
And turned to Archibald, my safe old bear,
Whose woollen eyes looked sad or glad at me,
Whose ample forehead I could wet with tears,
Whose half moon ears received my confidence,
Who made me laugh, who never let me down.
I used to wait for hours to see him move,
Convinced that he could breathe. One dreadful day
They hid him from me as a punishment:
Sometimes the desolation of that loss
Comes back to me and I must go upstairs
To see him in the sawdust, so to speak,
Safe and returned to his idolator.

From *Summoned by Bells*

Archie and the Strict Baptists

By Sir John Betjeman

here once was an elderly bear whose name was Archibald Ormsby-Gore. He had a companion, Jumbo, who was even older than he was. Jumbo had not much character or expression. But Archie had a lot and Archie's religion was Strict Baptist.

Archie lived at Garrard's Farm, Uffington, Berks. He liked it there very much as he only had to cross a field or two from the house to reach a Strict Baptist chapel. He used to ride over slowly on a hedgehog.

53

He always sat in the same high pew in the chapel. It had an Aneucapnic lamp fixed on a post. The lamp shone on his hymn book and on his aged head on winter evenings.

Two Aneucapnic lamps were on either side of the pulpit from which the Pastor preached, sometimes for five hours without stopping. The longer the sermon, the more Archie liked it.

Sometimes, when there was no Pastor supplied, Archie would preach himself. He went on for eight or nine hours until the chapel was empty and only the Aneucapnics were left to listen to him.

Archie was also an archaeologist, so he was quite happy on weekdays. He used to ride out on his hedgehog, carrying a spade. With this he used to dig up molehills, which, he considered, were the graves of baby Druids.

One day the family left the house at Uffington which was so nice and near the chapel.

They moved to another house high up on the downs in a tiny village called Farnborough. Archie preferred Farnborough in one way because there was no public house. He disapproved of public houses. There had been four in Uffington. But in another way he was sorry for the change because the nearest Strict Baptist chapel was seven miles away, down in the Vale.

For days at a stretch, Archie sat in a dark cupboard with no one to talk to but his rather characterless old friend, Jumbo. He felt unhappy and forgotten.

Through the open window, Archie would hear the bells calling people to church. They did not make him want to go to church, because he disapproved of church. But they *did* make him want to go to chapel.

And there he was, in the highest room of the house, locked up in a horrid 'utility' cupboard. There weren't even any Druidic remains for him to visit on weekdays. All around were just windy, empty hills.

And all the time, away down in the Vale was the homely little Strict Baptist chapel, where he longed to be. It stood among pollarded willows.

One evening somebody came to look in the cupboard where Archie and Jumbo lived, carrying an Aneucapnic lamp. The memories the lamp stirred up in the poor old animal were more than he could bear. He determined to go to chapel – somehow.

So when no one was about, he went down to the kitchen. He opened the kitchen-table drawer, which had brown paper in it, and, sitting happily on the table under the flypaper, he cut out for himself some brown paper wings.

Then he went to the edge of the downs and jumped.

The few people in Wantage market-place who were not at church were surprised to see a bear, with brown paper wings, flying over the town.

The chapel in the Vale was not quite so nice as the Uffington one. The pews were lower. The lamps were the more modern double-burner, chimney type, and not Aneucapnic. There were fewer people. But it was Strict Baptist and that was what really mattered.

Archie sat in the front with his brown paper wings beside him.

And in the gathering darkness, when service was over, Archie flew back to Farnborough. He could just see the outline of the church tower and the Wellingtonia in the garden away on top of the downs. It was heavy flying and his brown paper wings crackled.

He landed on the parapet by his attic window and took off his wings one at a time.

Back in the cupboard, Archie put his wings down beside Jumbo and spent the rest of the week telling him about the sermon. He flies to chapel every Sunday now and has nearly converted Jumbo to being a Strict Baptist, too.

The Night Ride

By Aingelda Ardizzone

 This story was first published in 1973, with illustrations by Edward Ardizzone.

Dandy, Kate and Tiny Teddy had lain forgotten in a dark cupboard for a long time. The children they belonged to had grown up and no longer played with them.

Then, one day just before Christmas, they were taken out of the cupboard and thrown into the dustbin.

Night came and it was dark and uncomfortable in the dustbin. But at dawn a chink of light shone through the gap between the bin and the lid.

The toys gazed sadly around them and wondered how they could get out.

Kate saw an old dish-mop. Dandy found a broken umbrella and Tiny Teddy a wooden spoon with a very long handle. Together they jumped up and down and pushed the lid off the dustbin. It fell off with a tremendous clatter.

Dandy lifted Tiny Teddy up. He climbed onto the edge of the bin and wriggled out. He slid down to the ground and waited by some flower-pots.

Then Kate and Dandy jumped out of the bin. They rested for a while and then began to look around.

In the hedge behind them they found an old toy engine. It was rusty here and there where the paint had worn off but the wheels were still strong.

The toys were very excited. They set to work at once to pull the engine out of the hedge. This was not too difficult once they had cleared the leaves and long grass that had grown around it.

The toys leapt onto the engine. 'I'll be the driver,' said Dandy, buttoning up his jacket. 'We will look for somewhere to live.'

The engine started to move very slowly and then it began to go faster and faster down the road.

Darkness fell but the toys were enjoying the ride so much that they did not want to stop. The moon rose and cast a silvery light over the fields.

On and on they rattled through villages and market towns.

After a while the toys began to feel tired and blown about by the cold wind. They longed to be safe and warm indoors.

Dandy was wondering which way to go and where they could stop, when they heard a strange roaring noise. It was the sound of a big diesel train coming nearer and nearer.

Then the little engine stopped with a terrific jolt beside a level-crossing gate.

The lights were on in the level-crossing keeper's house.

The toys could see a little girl looking out of a window, waiting to see the train go by. In the room behind her was a Christmas tree, covered with tinsel and pretty lights.

The little girl could scarcely believe her eyes when she saw the bent toy engine outside with Dandy, Kate and Tiny Teddy sitting on it. She ran out into the night to make sure she wasn't dreaming.

And there she found the bedraggled doll and the teddy bears and a battered toy engine.

The little girl picked them up one by one and carried them all indoors.

She tidied them up and played with them by the Christmas tree.

Although she had plenty of new toys, these were the ones she liked most of all.

Dandy, Kate and Tiny Teddy were happy in their new home. And when the litle girl gave them rides round the house on the toy engine, they always remembered their exciting ride through the night.

Bears

By Eulia Smith-Zimman

I love my Teddy Bear
He's such a friendly fellow,
His fur, beautiful and soft,
Is neither brown nor yellow.
He plays but never quarrels with me,
And keeps me gay and jolly,
And I don't have to punish him
As often as my dolly.
He's such a quiet little chap,
No impish schemes he hatches,
He never barks, he has no fleas,
At least he never scratches.

58

A Puzzling Question

By Shirley Isherwood

One evening, when Edward James was sitting in the kitchen, he suddenly thought, where was I, before I was living in this house with Mr Manders? He went to find Mr Manders to ask him.

Mr Manders was planting begonias in a flowerbed.

'Where was I, before I was here?' asked Edward James.

'You were sitting in the kitchen,' said Mr Manders. 'Where was I *before* I was sitting in the kitchen?' said Edward James. 'Before my breakfast – before *anything!*'

Mr Manders said that he didn't know. He found Edward James's question very puzzling, and went for a walk by himself to think about it. He walked right across the field, but he couldn't remember a time when Edward James had not been there.

Mr Manders went back to the kitchen. 'Think hard, Edward James,' he said. 'Try to remember where you were before you were here.'

Edward James thought very hard. He thought that he could remember last Tuesday, he said, but he wasn't sure.

'Try harder,' said Mr Manders. So Edward James tried harder – and he did remember last Tuesday.

'I was here,' he said. 'Where was I before that?'

Mr Manders got out a pad and a pencil on the table, and went out into the garden. Where *was* Edward James before he was here, thought Mr Manders. And then he thought, where was *I* before I was here? He thought as hard as he could – but he couldn't remember. Faster and faster he walked, as he tried to remember the mysterious time before he had lived with Edward James in the house by the stream.

'Why can't I remember it?' he said, as he went round and round, with Edward James trotting behind him. It was like trying to remember where he had put his gloves – sometimes he almost had the answer, and then he lost it again.

'Where *was* I?' he shouted, holding up his paws to the night sky. Then he looked at his paws, and turned them this way and that. They were a bit battered, and the velvet had worn thin in places. They are old paws, thought Mr Manders, but they are still good paws.

'I have been here a long time,' he said to Edward James. 'So much has happened to me that I can't remember it.' Then he looked at Edward James's paw. It was small and new, and firmly stuffed. 'But you haven't been here a long time,' he said. 'So you haven't got a lot to remember.'

But Edward James still wanted to know the answer to his question, and he stood in the field, staring at Mr Manders.

'I don't know,' said Mr Manders. 'I can't remember how we met – or anything.'

He took Edward James's paw, and led him back over the field and through the gap in the fence. 'But we *did* meet,' he said, 'and that's the most important thing.'

They went down the path in silence. The kitchen door stood open, and the flames that burned in the little iron stove shone brightly, and lit up the room. It looked warm and welcoming. 'I think we were here,' said Mr Manders. 'I think we have always been here.'

'Will we be here forever?' said Edward James.

'I expect so,' said Mr Manders.

My Teddy Bear

By Jeffrey S. Forman

Lines written to celebrate the bear's seventy-fifth birthday.

He sits upon his pillowed throne
A joyous smile upon his face.
And though his ears might seem outgrown
He carries them with pride and grace.

He's never cross or quick to carp.
A friend in need he is to me.
When human tongues are mean and sharp
My teddy gives me sympathy.

To him I always bare my soul.
He lifts me when I'm feeling low.
And when I brag and miss my goal
He never says, 'I told you so.'

My friends may titter gleefully
And some may tease, but I don't care.
I hope that I will never be
Too old to love my Teddy Bear.

Little Tommy Tittlemouse in the Bethnal
Green Museum, although well into his
seventies, still receives a birthday card
each year from 'Father'.

Bully Bear Goes to a Wedding

By Peter Bull

On the morning of the *Worshipful Company of Peanut Eaters' Annual Luncheon*, Bully Bear set out in his Full Regalia to catch the bus.

As he was waiting, he saw a piece of paper lying in the road. It looked like a grand, but rather muddy invitation. 'Your Presents' he thought it began. Bully was KEEN on Presents, so he stood there puzzled . . . he heard a voice . . . 'Can I help, Sir?' Bully looked up to find a kindly Taxi Man leaning out of his cab. Bully Bear handed him the piece of paper. The Taxi Man was most impressed. 'Lord-luv-a-duck, you're going to be late. Nip in!' And in Bully nipped. He noticed a Great Many Persons in the street as they drove along. 'What a lot of presents they must be giving out,' thought Bully.

They drew up near a great building, with lots more Persons about.

'This is as far as I can take you, Sir. You will have to go the rest of the way on Shanks's Pony,' said the Taxi Man as he waved good-bye.

'Shanks's Pony, what could that nice man mean?' Bully pondered.

There were plenty of ponies about, rather large ones, but they were all being sat on by Military Men. So he walked, and climbed up a great many steps, puff-puff. . . Until he found himself at the feet of a little girl, carrying a bouquet of flowers, who said to him sharply, '*You're* late. Take the train at once, take the train!'

'Whatever next?' thought Bully. 'Taxis, Ponies, and now Trains. I see no trains!' Firmly, the cross little girl put the edge of a very long dress in his paw, cuffed him quite hard, and pushed him forward. Bully was swept along, in a sea of pretty shoes and flouncy frocks, to the sound of the grandest band he'd ever heard. There was also singing. Meanwhile, at Bully Bear Lodge (Residential Accommodation for Select Bears), the Lodgers were watching the Great Event on the television set.

Suddenly, a great shout went up. 'It's Bully! It's our Bully!' they cried. 'He might have told us where he was going in all that posh get up.'

Bertram Bibblecombe Billyho Bear

By Ivy O. Eastwick

Bertram Bibblecombe Billyho Bear
Went on a Friday to Faradown Fair,
Rode on the roundabouts,
Swung on the swings,
Bought candy-floss, ice-cream
And toffees and things.
And then he decided
To buy some sweet honey,
But oh my! by then
He'd spent all his money,
So Bertram Bibblecombe Billyho Bear
Turned and walked home from Faradown Fair.

Tubby Ted's New Chimney

By Ursula Hourihane

 *Tubby Ted is a small, fat teddy bear who lives in a yellow caravan with red wheels. His friend, Mr Nogs, an old dapple-grey horse, grazes in the field outside.*

The summer was nearly over and Tubby Ted and Mr Nogs were making the most of every sunny day that came. They played down by the pond and they went for long rambles over the fields to pick blackberries and nuts and look for mushrooms. Tubby Ted had put a few nails in Mr Nogs' little shed to make sure that its wooden sides and roof would keep the old horse snug and dry all through the winter months ahead.

'It looks a bit like rain tonight,' Mr Nogs said as the sun went down in a very angry red sky. 'It's a good job you fixed up my shed so carefully, Tubs. . .'

They said goodnight and Tubby Ted was soon snug and warm in his cosy caravan.

'There's a wind getting up,' he said to himself as he lay snuggling under the bed-clothes a little later. 'I'm glad old Nogs will be safe in his shed. The nights are getting too chilly for him out in the field now.' Then he sang a few little songs to himself and fell asleep.

But while Tubby Ted was sleeping quietly in his bunk and old Mr Nogs was dreaming away peacefully in his shed, a great storm arose. The wind came clattering round the caravan and the rain beat down on the roof, louder and louder. Tubby Ted woke at last, wondering what all the noise could be. . .

WHOO – OOO! blew the wind through the keyhole. WHOO – OOO! it called through the window shutters. It shook the little yellow caravan and the rain spattered down the chimney. Then there was a wilder blow than ever and a clatter and a bang and a fearful CRASH!

'My goodness!' cried Tubby Ted sitting up in bed in a hurry. 'Whatever's blown down? I should think it must be the old oak tree by the noise it made!'

But it wasn't till morning came and the storm had blown away that Tubby Ted could see what had happened. The wind had blown off his shiny tin chimney-pot! Tubby Ted was upset. And so was Mr Nogs. . .

'Now what shall we do, Nogs?' said Tubby Ted. 'I should think a new chimney would cost a terrible lot of money and we've not got much in our money-box, have we?'

He fetched out their smart red letter-box with its wide slit for the money to go through. But when they managed to empty it at last there was only two shillings and threepence altogether. Mr Nogs shook his big head sadly.

'Two shillings and threepence won't be nearly enough money to buy a new chimney-pot.'

Suddenly Tubby Ted clapped his paws.

'Got it,' he shouted. . . 'We'll sell things out of our field, Nogs. We've got lots of nice things here that people would be glad to buy.'

Mr Nogs gave a sort of grunt. 'What sort of things do you mean?' he asked. 'We can't sell the caravan things, can we?'

Tubby Ted laughed. 'My goodness, no!' he said. 'I mean things like flowers and mushrooms and blackberries and nuts. We've plenty of these haven't we? We could do a good trade.'

'PRRRH! Of course we have,' whinnied Mr Nogs delightedly. 'Clever old Tubs! We'll make pounds and pounds of money. Hurrah!'

It was hard work collecting all the things they needed to sell, but Tubby Ted and Mr Nogs didn't let that bother them a bit.

'We'll have to put a notice by the gate to say we're opening a shop,' said Tubby Ted. 'You pull the table there while I write it out, Nogs.'

They turned the table upside down so that Mr Nogs could drag it across the field more easily, and Tubby Ted went into the caravan to write the notice.

'Oh dear,' he said as he got the red and blue pencils and a big sheet of paper out of the cupboard. 'Now I've let Nogs take the table away and I've got nothing to write on.'

He lay flat on the floor in the end and the writing looked a bit wobbledy, but anyone could see that it said:

THINGS FOR SALE
COME AND BY NISE FRESH
FLOWERS AND FROOT

I'm afraid Tubby Ted didn't spell it all quite right, as you can see, but people must have understood because they stopped when they saw the notice and the table with its collection of good things for sale. By the end of the day Tubby Ted and Mr Nogs had sold every single thing and their money box was so full they had to get a jar to put the last lot of money in.

'We've got plenty to buy our new chimney-pot, haven't we?' cried Tubby Ted excitedly.

And indeed they had. There was even enough left over to buy a lantern to hang outside the front door.

Honey Bear

By Elizabeth Lang

There was a big bear
Who lived in a cave.
His greatest love
Was honey.
He had twopence a week,
Which he never could save,
So he never had any money.
I bought him a money box
Red and round,
In which to put
His money.
He saved and saved
Till he got a pound,
Then he spent it all
on honey.

Birro Goes Flying

By Hans Andreus

 *This extract comes from Holland, from the book 'The Bear Who Stood on his Head', translated by Patricia Crampton. Later in the story Birro does experience flying – in an aeroplane.*

Martin and his teddy bear Birro were playing in the garden. They were looking at the birds.

Martin watched with a deep frown.

'Why can't I fly?' he asked.

'Because you're not a bird, you're a boy,' said Birro.

'But what if I flapped my arms up and down very quickly?'

'Try it,' said Birro.

Martin moved his arms up and down very vigorously and took a leap but nothing happened. He stayed on the ground. His frown grew even deeper and he pulled an old crate out of the shed. He climbed onto it and jumped off, flapping his arms up and down again. But he did not fly in the air. He landed in the grass and actually fell over onto his knees.

'Ow!' said Martin, rubbing his knees. Then he looked seriously at his teddy bear Birro and asked: 'Why can't bears fly?'

'Because we're not birds, we're bears,' said Birro.

'Are you absolutely sure you can't?' said Martin.

Birro sighed and clambered onto the crate.

'Look out, I'm coming!' he cried, jumping and flapping his arms up and down. Of course Birro fell to the ground just as Martin except that the bear fell backwards instead of forwards.

'See, I can't fly,' said Birro, 'and I must say I don't think this game is much fun.'

'The thing is,' said Martin, 'that if you had been able to fly, you would have been able to tell me all about it later – about what flying feels like.'

Senior Under Officer Edward Bear from the Royal Military Academy, Sandhurst, knows exactly what flying feels like having jumped for twenty-one years with the Sandhurst Edward Bear Parachute Club.

Teddy Robinson as he is today, still much loved by three generations
of the Robinson family.

Teddy Robinson's Night Out

By Joan G. Robinson

Teddy Robinson was a nice, big, comfortable, friendly teddy bear. He had light brown fur and kind, brown eyes, and he belonged to a little girl called Deborah. He was Deborah's favourite teddy bear, and Deborah was Teddy Robinson's favourite little girl, so they got on very well together, and wherever one of them went the other one usually went, too.

One Saturday afternoon Teddy Robinson and Deborah looked out of the window and saw that the sun was shining and the almond-tree in the garden was covered with pink blossom.

'That's nice,' said Deborah. 'We can play out there. We will make our house under the little pink tree, and you can get brown in the sun, Teddy Robinson.'

So she took out a little tray with the dolls' tea-set on it, and a blanket to sit on, and the toy telephone in case anyone rang them up, and she laid all the things out on the grass under the tree. Then she fetched a colouring book and some chalks for herself, and a book of nursery rhymes for Teddy Robinson.

Deborah lay on her tummy and coloured the whole of an elephant and half a Noah's ark, and Teddy Robinson stared hard at a picture of Humpty-Dumpty and tried to remember the words. He couldn't really read but he loved pretending to.

'Hump, hump, humpety-hump,' he said to himself over and over again; and then, 'Hump, hump, humpety-hump, Deborah's drawing an elephump.'

'Oh, Teddy Robinson,' said Deborah, 'don't think so loud – I can't hear myself chalking.' Then, seeing him still bending over his book, she said, 'Poor boy, I expect you're tired. It's time for your rest now.' And she laid him down flat on his back so that he could look up into the sky.

71

At that moment there was a loud *rat-tat* on the front door and a long ring on the door-bell. Deborah jumped up and ran indoors to see who it could be, and Teddy Robinson lay back and began to count the number of blossoms he could see in the almond-tree. He couldn't count more than four because he only had two arms and two legs to count on, so he counted up to four a great many times over, and then he began counting backward, and the wrong way round, and any way round that he could think of, and sometimes he put words in between his counting, so that in the end it went something like this:

'One, two, three, four,
someone knocking at the door.
One, four, three, two,
open the door and how d'you do?
Four, two, three, one,
isn't it nice to lie in the sun?
One, two, four, three,
underneath the almond-tree.'

And he was very happy counting and singing to himself for quite a long time.

Then Teddy Robinson noticed that the sun was going down and there were long shadows in the garden. It looked as if it must be getting near bedtime.

Deborah will come and fetch me soon, he thought; and he watched the birds flying home to their nests in the trees above him.

A blackbird flew quite close to him and whistled and chirped, 'Good night, teddy bear.'

'Good night, bird,' said Teddy Robinson and waved an arm at him.

Then a snail came crawling past.

'Are you sleeping out tonight? That will be nice for you,' he said. 'Good night, teddy bear.'

'Good night, snail,' said Teddy Robinson, and he watched it

crawl slowly away into the long grass.

She will come and fetch me soon, he thought. It must be getting quite late.

But Deborah didn't come and fetch him. Do you know why? She was fast asleep in bed!

This is what had happened. When she had run to see who was knocking at the front door, Deborah had found Uncle Michael standing on the doorstep. He had come in his new car, and he said there was just time to take her out for a ride if she came quickly. . . By the time they reached home Deborah was half asleep, and Mummy had bundled her into bed before she had time to really wake up again and remember about Teddy Robinson still being in the garden.

He didn't know all this, of course, but he guessed something unusual must have happened to make Deborah forget about him.

Soon a little wind blew across the garden, and down fluttered some blossom from the almond-tree. It fell right in the middle of Teddy Robinson's tummy.

'Thank you,' he said, 'I like pink flowers for a blanket.'

The next-door kitten came padding softly through the grass and rubbed against him gently.

'You *are* out late,' she said.

'Yes, I think I'm sleeping out tonight,' said Teddy Robinson.

'Are you?' said the kitten. 'You'll love that. I did it once. I'm going to do it a lot oftener when I'm older. Perhaps I'll stay out tonight.'

But just then a window opened in the house next door and a voice called, 'Puss! Puss! Puss! Come and have your fish! fish! fish!' and the kitten scampered off as fast as she could go.

Teddy Robinson heard the window shut down and then everything was quiet again.

The sky grew darker and darker blue, and soon the stars came out. Teddy Robinson lay and stared at them without blinking, and they twinkled and shone and winked at him as if they were surprised to see a teddy bear lying in the garden.

And after a while they began to sing to him, a very soft and

sweet and far-away little song, to the tune of *Rock-a-Bye Baby*, and it went something like this:

> '*Rock-a-Bye Teddy, go to sleep soon,*
> *We will be watching, so will the moon,*
> *When you awake with dew on your paws,*
> *Down will come Debbie and take you indoors.*'

. . . Very early in the morning a blackbird whistled, then another blackbird answered, and then all the birds in the garden opened their beaks and twittered and cheeped and sang. And Teddy Robinson woke up. . .

Then a moment later Teddy Robinson heard a little shuffling noise in the grass behind him, and there was Deborah out in the garden with bare feet, and in her pyjamas!

She picked him up and hugged him and kissed him and whispered to him very quietly, and then she ran through the wet grass and in at the kitchen door and up the stairs into her own room. A minute later she and Teddy Robinson were snuggled down in her warm little bed.

'You poor, poor boy,' she whispered as she stroked his damp fur. 'I never meant to leave you out all night. Oh, you poor, poor boy.'

But Teddy Robinson whispered back, 'I aren't a poor boy at all. I was camping out, and it was lovely.' And then he tried to tell her all about the blackbird, and the snail, and the kitten, and the stars. But because it was really so very early in the morning, and Deborah's bed was really so very warm and cosy, they both got drowsy; and before he had even got to the part about the stars singing their song to him both Teddy Robinson and Deborah were fast asleep.

Traditional Playground Rhymes

Round and round the garden,
Like a teddy bear,
One step, two step . . .
Tickle you under there!

Teddy bear, teddy bear turn around.
Teddy bear, teddy bear touch the ground.
Teddy bear, teddy bear go up stairs.
Teddy bear, teddy bear say your prayers.
Teddy bear, teddy bear switch off the light.
Teddy bear, teddy bear say good night.

Teddy on the railway
Picking up stones,
Along came an engine
And broke Teddy's bones.
'Oh!' said Teddy,
'That's not fair.'
'Pooh,' said the engine driver,
'I don't care.'

75

Teddy

By Brian Hick

After sixty-one years of loving disinterest
Repaired yet retired to lurk in attics
In damp plastic boxes of last season's dresses
He returned to daylight more faded than ever
To win the school prize for the oldest bear.

The sepia photo of my two-year-old mother
Beaming plumply by her brand new bear
Shows little resemblance to the patched bald figure
Who sits before me, staring cockeyed
With the two black buttons I sewed as a child;

An over-large nose, bright red and padded
To replace the hessian eaten by moths,
And tartan paws, themselves now faded,
But once the latest fashion in bears;

A lopsided patch in his lefthand side
Covers the wound of a vital operation
To save his life from a rusty squeaker
And fatten him up on a diet of stockings.

My constant companion in earlier days,
I cried all night in my hospital cot
When moved by a nurse who did not understand
My fear I would never see him again.

I'm not a hoarder but in eight house moves
He has gone with me, along with my wife
And successive children, journeying calmly
From loft to attic, biding his time,
Knowing his moment of glory would come

As it did, with an Easter Egg prize for Lucy
And a commendation for an ancient bear
Who will never grace an attic again.

77

T.R. Arrives

By Terrance Dicks

T.R. Bear is a tough, robust character who arrives unexpectedly in a parcel from America, and as Jimmy discovers, as soon as he unwraps him, he is certainly no ordinary teddy bear.

At last inside the box there was a bear.

It was a teddy bear. But somehow it wasn't quite like any other bear he'd ever seen.

It was smallish and broad shouldered.

Instead of the gentle, amiable air of most teddy bears, this bear had a kind of determined, almost scowling, expression. This bear looked tough – despite the fact that it was wearing glasses, small, perfectly round ones with black wire frames.

'Surely a bear can't need glasses,' thought Jimmy.

Then he realized that the spectacles had no glass in them.

There was a letter on top of the bear.

Jimmy took it out of the box and handed it to his mother. 'Read it out, Mum.'

His mother looked at the letter. 'It's from your Uncle Colin in Connecticut.'

She began to read:

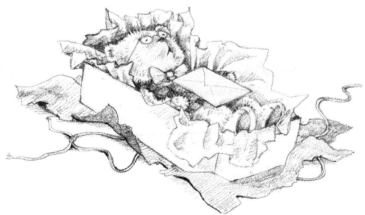

'Dear Jimmy,
We found this teddy bear in the attic of the house we
just bought over here. As we bought the house and all its contents,
I guess he's ours. As you know, our kids are all grown up so we
thought you might like to have him.
All the best to you and the family.
Love,
Uncle Colin

'Oh, there's a P.S. According to the label on the box, his name is Theodore Roosevelt Bear. Bit of a mouthful, that. You could call him T.R. for short.'

Jimmy looked down at the bear.

Lying in his box of tissue paper, the bear looked rather as if it was asleep in bed.

Just to try out the sound of it, Jimmy said, 'T.R. Bear!'

The bear woke up. Its eyes opened wide behind the round spectacle-frames. It yawned and stretched, and sat up, looking the astonished Jimmy straight in the eye.

'Hi there, kid,' said T.R. Bear. 'How ya doing?'

Everyone stared at the teddy bear in amazement.

Jimmy was just as surprised as everyone else – but he wasn't too surprised to notice something else.

He saw that the teddy bear was just as surprised as the people around it. It looked round with an air of utter astonishment, made a noise that sounded something like 'Urrk!' and collapsed backwards into the box.

There was a moment of silence.

Jimmy's father said, 'Amazing! What will they think of next?'

'But it *talked*,' said his mother. 'And it sat up!'

'Voice activated tape recorder probably,' said George airily. He always liked to have the explanation for everything.

Jenny said, 'Try it again, Jimmy.'

'Hello, T.R. Bear!' said Jimmy.

The teddy bear didn't move or speak. It lay in its box, clearly a toy bear and nothing more.

George said, 'I imagine the battery must have run down. After all, if it's been stuck away in an attic for ages. . .'

They all prodded and poked the bear for a bit, but they couldn't feel anything that felt like machinery inside.

George wanted to take it apart and try and mend it, but Jimmy wouldn't let him.

After a bit, everyone lost interest and drifted off.

As she went out Jenny whispered, 'Never mind, Jimmy. I daresay he'll talk again when he feels like it.'

Left alone, Jimmy examined the bear a bit longer. Once or twice he tried shouting 'Hello T.R.!' very loudly, but it didn't do any good. Finally he put T.R. on the shelf, between two of his other toys. One was a teddy bear called Edward that he'd had since he was very small.

The other was a rag doll called Sally Ann. She was Jenny's doll really. Although Jenny felt she'd outgrown her, she was too fond of the doll either to throw or give it away.

So Sally Ann had moved into Jimmy's room. Jenny said she would be company for Edward.

For ages now they had sat on the toy shelf side by side. The long, wide shelf ran along the end of Jimmy's room, just above the bookcase, next to the cage with the gerbils. By raising his head a little Jimmy could see the rag doll and the teddy bear sitting side by side, just before he went to sleep. . .

He must have fallen asleep and woken up again. He was lying in bed in a sort of drifting doze when he heard a drawling voice say, 'But my dear fellow, really! How could you?' Somehow he knew at once that it was Edward Bear speaking. Edward was a very aristocratic looking teddy bear, tall and thin. As a matter of fact, the voice sounded very like Prince Charles.

A second voice said reproachfully. 'You spoke – in front of humans. It's breaking all the rules.'

This was a female voice, very clipped and efficient, and

Jimmy knew at once it just had to be Sally Ann.

Jimmy lifted his head a little and half-opened his eyes. Then he lay quite still in bed, listening hard.

He heard the deep, rumbling voice of T.R. 'Listen, give me a break! You guys never heard of jet lag? For years I get stuck in an attic, then I get thrown in a box and whizzed over the Atlantic. So naturally, when I wake up I'm a little confused. Could happen to anybody.'

'Nonsense,' said Sally Ann severely. 'The rules are perfectly clear. No moving or talking unless the humans are asleep, and we're all alone.'

'One simply must have proper standards of behaviour, old chap,' said Edward severely.

T.R. sounded as if he was getting impatient. 'Okay, okay,' he rumbled. 'I apologise. It should never have happened, but it did, and I can't make it un-happen.'

'Now the humans know you can talk,' said Sally Ann worriedly.

'They might even begin to guess about the rest of us.'

T.R. wasn't worried. 'Listen, lady, let me tell you something about humans. They believe what they *wanna* believe. Likewise, they don't believe what they *don't* wanna believe. And no human wants to believe in talking toys. You saw what happened. They've already convinced themselves that I'm some kind of mechanical gizmo. Pretty soon they'll forget the whole thing. Trust me.'

'Well, I just hope you're right, old fellow,' said Edward. 'We'll just have to overlook it – after all, you are an *American* bear. I suppose we should expect some strange behaviour.'

'Oh yeah? And what's so strange about an American bear?'

'Teddy bears are British,' said Edward positively. 'Everyone knows that.'

From *Enter T.R.*

Ludvig Bear

By Delma

My favourite bear
Has prickly hair –
And ears that point to heaven.
He's up at six,
Eats cereal mix –
And dozes then 'til 'leven.

At ten to one
It's honey bun –
And fizzy ginger beer.
A yachting cap,
An ocean map –
And walking on the pier.

At ten to four,
The café door –
Is beckoning for tea;
(The sandwiches are rather big,
Smelly cheese and squelchy fig –
And crumbs on either knee.)

At half past five
He checks his line –
And counts his honey bees;
Watches babies
Learning to fly –
(And warns of flying fleas).

My favourite bear
Has prickly hair –
And ears that point to heaven.
As choosing next
His cocoa jug,
He CAREFULLY fills his bed-time mug –
And sleeps from ten to 'leven.

Odd and Elsewhere

By James Roose-Evans

This introductory piece is from the first of seven books about a small bear called Odd and his friend, Elsewhere, inseparable comrades in a series of exciting adventures.

Sprawled in a corner, the small bear could see the removal van drive away. Everybody had gone and he was left alone in the empty house. He was feeling extra sorry for himself because he had also caught a cold. For as long as he had known Odd had never had any trousers, only a blue and white striped shirt which, by dint of tugging, he had managed to stretch into a skirt or kilt – but still he felt very draughty. . .

83

'The odds are,' he murmured to himself, 'that I am the only person left in this house, and what could be odder than that?' He paused for a moment, cocking his head towards a reflection of himself, encountered that moment in a piece of broken mirror tilted against the wall.

'Indeed,' he murmured sagely to his reflected self, 'what could be odder than Odd?'

'Or who?' came a voice at that moment.

Odd looked around the empty room. He felt like saying, 'Is there anybody there?' but decided this might sound a little odd.

'Dedadedadedadeda!' he sang tunelessly, unable to make up his mind.

'Odds and boddikins!' exclaimed the voice. 'Is that supposed to be an ode or an oddity? Come and help me get out of here!'

The sing-song voice seemed to come from inside a tall cupboard. Knotting together the tail ends of his shirt, Odd ambled over to contemplate the problem of opening a cupboard, the handle of which was too high for him to reach.

'If you pull and I push, you'll find the door is only stuck,' said the voice.

'Ah, but don't you see,' explained Odd, 'except that you can't see – of course, I see that – that I'm too short to reach the handle. Now, let me see!'

All these 'sees' were beginning to make him see-sick, so he put his paws behind his back and began to pace up and down. Suddenly he noticed the flex of the electric light hanging from one wall.

Taking hold of the switch he walked backwards and took a running jump at the cupboard. If only he could catch hold of the door handle as he flew past. . .

Crash! bang! ouch! Odd lay on the floor battered and bruised.

'Odds and boddikins!' screamed the voice within. 'There's no need to batter in the door!'

84

. . . It was at this moment that Odd's nose started to become unstitched, and he sat there, feeling distinctly sorry for himself and very much at odds with the world, staring cross-eyed at his running nose.

The long flex, weighted by the switch at the end, swung back and forth, like the tail of an angry cat.

'The problem,' muttered Odd to himself, now determined not to be beaten, 'is how to open that door.'

From within the cupboard there was not a sound. Odd began to be alarmed in case whoever was inside had suffocated. What could he do?

He padded over to the flex and absent-mindedly pressed the switch on and off. If only he could loop the flex around the handle and then tug, he should be able to open the door.

He tried once, he tried twice. 'If at first you don't succeed, try, try again!' he muttered to himself, tugging away. One final jerk and the door of the cupboard opened. At the same moment the ceiling cracked, the light socket fell out, and Odd lay buried under a pile of plaster! He sat in the middle of the room, like a snowman, his nose unthreading.

'Atchoo! Atchoo!' came from the cupboard as the dust from the plaster filled the room. Odd turned to peer through the sudden fog and there, hanging upside down by one leg – the foot caught in a hook on the upper shelf – was a circus clown.

The clown had bright red wool hair, a red beaked nose and white face, beady black eyes, a yellow bow round the neck with a jewelled brooch in the centre, a red shirt covered with white spots, and candy-striped trousers!

'Atchoo!' sneezed the clown.

Odd, who still felt a little dazed by his fall, sat staring. Suddenly the upside-down clown opened one eye and winked at him.

'You look like a chimpanzee!' observed Odd, then blushed brown because that sounded rather rude.

'So would you!' retorted the clown, 'if you were stuck up here and couldn't get down. Instead of making such footling and fatuous remarks, why don't you find a pole or something and push me off this hook?'

'But you'd break your neck!' exclaimed Odd.

'Not I!' answered the clown. 'For Falls, various and spectacular! All Jelly-Rolls, Back-Somersaults, Head-Stands, Hand-Stands, Cart-Wheels, you can't touch us! Why, we used to have all our bones broken before we were born!'

'That's all very well for you,' retorted Odd, 'but I'm bruised all over!'

He decided the clown was rather conceited. . . Besides, now that he looked, the clown did not seem to be very uncomfortable. Indeed, he seemed to be enjoying his topsy-turvy state, and was singing to himself, swinging gently from side to side.

As the clown sang louder and louder, so he swung from side to side more and more vigorously. Suddenly his foot was loosened by the violent movement, and for the second time that day Odd found himself buried under an avalanche!

'Don't you think we ought to introduce ourselves?' he said, extricating himself from the tangle of arms and legs. 'I'm Odd,' he added.

'You can say that again!' chuckled the clown. He sat up abruptly, throwing one floppy leg over the other, and leaned back on his hands, which were covered with white gloves. 'I'm Elsewhere!' he said, loftily.

Outside in the street a barrel organ was playing, and in a moment Elsewhere had pulled Odd to his feet, and both were dancing round the room.

'Dedadedadedadeda!' sang Odd loudly.

'Lalalalalalala!' echoed Elsewhere, as they revolved faster and faster until, out of breath, they fell on the floor, laughing and giggling with delight.

'After all,' thought Odd, 'I'm not alone any more.'

The real Odd and his inseparable friend Elsewhere.

King, Eli and Evans as they are today. Queen and Jarvis, alas, succumbed to moth some years ago.

King

By Simon Theobalds

He wasn't called King when we first met.
He belonged to my sister before me
But you could tell by the way his eyes were set
That he was not just any old pet
But a wise old bear – a really good bet
To put in charge of the nursery.

He wasn't the kind of bear to dress up
Or involve in let's pretend.
He was in charge, and when he was there
Everyone else was aware of the bear
With his steady gaze and unwinking stare
That would see things through to the end.

He wasn't sad but he did not smile.
He took things in his stride.
A serious far off look had he.
He never said very much to me
(That's because he was thinking you see)
And he had Queen by his side.

She was less of a bear
But fit to be seen.
She had more fur
But her eyes would blur
(I never knew what he saw in her)
But none the less she was Queen.

There were others around to do the jobs
That needed to be done:
Prime Minister Jarvis to govern the land,
The Army had Eli to lead the band,
The Navy – Evans' steady hand
But they knew that King was the special one.

It's a different world King lives in now,
And he gets a lot more rest.
Sometimes he is picked up by my son
Or one of his sisters wanting fun
But very soon their play is done
And they go back to those they love best.

Eli and Evans are still around
And no doubt shake their heads
Over micro-chip toys,
With all their noise
– The kind of things that modern boys
Now want to have in their beds.

A row of teddy bears sitting in a toyshop, all one size, all one price. Yet how different each is from the next. Some look gay, some look sad. Some look stand-offish, some look lovable. And one in particular, that one over there, has a specially endearing expression. Yes, that is the one we would like, please.

Christopher Milne in *The Enchanted Places*

The Shoe Shop Bears

By Margaret J. Baker

The Shoe Shop Bear books, written in the late '60s, conjure up a world of domestic practicality very different from the cosy, middle class nursery settings of some of the earlier teddy bear stories.

No bears could have had a happier home than Wellington Boots, Slippers and Socks had with the Trinkets at No. 1, Station Road, Slumber Lightly. In the small, terraced house, Simon and Bill and their sister, Audrey, gave the three bears every care and attention. Boots' golden fur was brushed and smoothed carefully over the thinning patches round his muzzle, and his back paws were padded with the best chamois-leather. There was never a speck of dust to tempt a hungry moth on Slippers' worn, honey-coloured fur, and Socks, though usually untidy, always had a fresh chocolate-box-ribbon bow washed and ironed by Audrey herself.

None of the bears was new. For most of their lives they had worked in the shoe shop in Cordwainer's Row, close to the Cathedral. They had been kept to amuse the younger customers during the fitting of their shoes. Polly Trinket, the children's elder sister, worked in the shoe shop too, and when the time came for the bears to retire she had given them a welcome into her own home.

But now there were a great many other things to interest the bears besides boots and shoes. The house was their first real home. As Boots often told the others, they were now house-holders with their own responsibilities.

Directly Mrs Trinket left for work Boots hurried from room to room setting all the shoes to rights. He crawled in search of bedroom slippers kicked into corners under the boys' bunk beds, and arranged all their puddle-boots neatly in pairs. Now and then he frowned over a scuffed toe or a loose sole or whistled quietly as he untangled a knotted lace. Afterwards he tidied the biscuit-box in which the shoe-brushes were kept and the tins of polish and velvet pads that Polly made specially from her young sister's out-grown Sunday dresses.

Slippers enjoyed living in the house even more than Boots and Socks. She was always happiest when the other bears were safe and warm. In the shoe shop she had always worried about their welfare. The danger from moths had troubled her most of all. Now it was a great relief to her that the children's mother shared her fears, and a drum of anti-moth liquid always stood ready on the kitchen dresser. In an emergency Slippers could squirt the liquid herself by pressing a knob with her paw.

Of all the rooms in the house Slippers liked the kitchen best. On the back door hung a wooden clock with hands that told the milkman and baker how many loaves or pints to leave. Once when Mrs Trinket had forgotten to set the hands to the right numbers the bears had done it for her themselves. On the dresser was an egg-timer and a pair of scales. If Boots sat on one end of the scales and Slippers and Socks perched on the other with a four-ounce weight the scales made an excellent see-saw. Inside the dresser was a mincing-machine, which Socks soon learnt to assemble all by himself. There was also an icing-bag for decorating cakes. They longed to try it with real icing-sugar, but it worked just as well with mashed potato left over from lunch.

Socks liked to play in the bathroom best of all. He was the smallest of all the bears, but, using both paws, he could turn on the bath-taps. Swinging to and fro on the bath-plug chain, with the water gushing close by, he felt like an acrobat performing over Niagara Falls.

'You shouldn't do it,' Slippers told him one day after he had fallen in. 'It wastes the water.'

'I'm not wasting it,' Socks insisted as she rubbed him dry. 'I'm cleaning the bath, and Boots said we ought to help.'

Sometimes Socks skated with one paw on a cake of wet soap, or he tobogganed down the end of the bath, pretending it was the glittering slope of a snow-covered mountain.

In the front room of No. 1, Station Road, was an upright rosewood piano. Photographs in real silver frames stood on top, with a vase filled with paper roses in the winter and real ones in the summer-time. When everyone was out, Slippers would sit at the piano and pick out tunes with one paw. She could manage most of *God Save the Queen* and a good deal of *Three Blind Mice*. Boots would usually oblige by sitting on the loud pedal, but he liked best of all to open the top of the piano and watch the hammers as they struck the wires.

Every afternoon the bears sat in the front room perched on the window-sill beside Mrs Trinket's maidenhair-fern in its pink and gold-fluted pot. Boots dozed while Socks and Slippers watched everything that went on in the road. No bears could have a better view.

Bananas

By Carey Blyton

Bananas
In pyjamas,
Are coming down the stairs,
Bananas
In pyjamas,
Are coming down in pairs;
Bananas in pyjamas,
Are chasing teddy bears –
'Cos on Tuesdays
They all try to
CATCH THEM UNAWARES.

The Teddy Bear

By L. H. Allen

Teddy Bear
Sat on a chair
With ham and jam
And plum and pear.

'This is queer,'
Said Teddy Bear.
'The more I eat
The less is there!'

Teddy Valena

By Brigid Keenan

Teddy Valena is quite a bit older than me. She had been new for my sister, but by the time I inherited her she had been around for about seven years, and was a respected member of the household, a personality in her own right. A measure of her status is that she was – and is – always known as Teddy Valena and never by any name shorter or cuter. I never looked on Teddy Valena as a cuddly toy, but rather as someone more mature and wiser than me, which made what happened later extra painful.

Perhaps nothing illustrates the wisdom about beauty being in the eye of the beholder better than the way children see their toys. We all know – we have all been – little people who can't go to bed without a piece of grimy blanket or a tattered toy clutched to the cheek. Teddy Valena was not fluffy like other bears, but smooth (some would call it bald), and in places the canvas of her skin was shiny with dirt. Her squeak had long since been silent, but the mechanism stuck out of her sagging body a bit. Her eyes had fallen out ages before I knew her, and we coloured around the pin holes where they had been with blue crayon. She was always nicely dressed because my sister made her clothes – she even had a ballet tutu – and though I realized that she was not conventionally pretty, I looked on her as a sophisticated *jolie laide*, an elegant woman of the world. In fact both Teddy Valena and I were women of the world in one sense because we were born in India – I in the Military Hospital at Ambala and Teddy Valena at the Army and Navy Stores in Bombay. When I was eight my family returned to England and then she and I became even closer if that was possible, for she was the only creature on earth, apart from my parents and sisters, who really knew what living in India had been like. Teddy Valena had shared the houses we'd lived in, the personalities involved in our lives, the pets we'd had – our whole family history.

About two years after we returned to England I was sent to boarding school, and to cheer me up my sister made Teddy Valena a miniature school uniform identical to mine. I went off with my courage bolstered up by my marvellously dressed toy. But at school they saw things differently – there was no beauty in the eyes of those merciless girls.

'WHAT'S THIS?' they shrieked in the dormitory on my first night, grabbing Teddy Valena off my pillow.

'It's my teddy bear,' I said shyly.

'TEDDY BEAR! This isn't a BEAR, this is a PIG,' they taunted, flinging her from one to another so that her blazer came flying open and started falling off her shoulders.

'And what's more,

it's a dirty old pig and it's probably got fleas. It's a flea pig. FLEA PIG! FLEA PIG! FLEA PIG!'

They tore off her clothes and threw her to and fro across the dormitory with me as another, desperate, pig in the middle, jumping to catch her and crying, and begging for her to be given back. I thought my heart would break at the hurt and humiliation they were inflicting on my beloved friend, who in all her life had never even been put to sit in an uncomfortable position. In the end they got bored with the game and threw her on the floor. I sobbed all night, hugging her close to comfort her.

Teddy Valena and I survived, and she belongs now to my eight-year-old daughter who loves her as much as I did. There is one change though – we do not take her out very much, and certainly never ever to school.

Here's something to love and something to tease,
Something to cuddle and something to squeeze,
Someone who'll stick thro' storm and fair,
A dear little, cute little Brown Teddy Bear.

Rhyme from an early postcard

Goodnight Ben

By Bernard Waber

I was invited to sleep at Reggie's house.
Was I happy!
I had never slept at a friend's house before.
But I had a problem.
It began when my sister said:
'Are you taking your teddy bear along?'
'Taking my teddy bear along!' I said.
'To my friend's house? Are you kidding?
That's the silliest thing I ever heard!
Of course, I'm not taking my teddy bear.'
And then she said:
'But you never slept without
your teddy bear before.
How will you feel sleeping without
your teddy bear for the very
first time? Hmmmmmmmmmmmmmmmm?'
'I feel fine.
I feel great.
I will probably love sleeping
without my teddy bear.
Just don't worry about it,' I said.
'Who's worried?' she said.
But now she had me
thinking about it.
Now, she really had me
thinking about it.
I began to wonder:
Suppose I won't like
sleeping without my teddy bear.
Suppose I just hate
sleeping without my teddy bear.

Should I take him?
'Take him,' said my mother.
'Take him,' said my father.
'But Reggie will laugh,' I said.
'He'll say I'm a baby.'
'He won't laugh,' said my mother.
'He won't laugh,' said my father.
'He'll laugh,' said my sister.
I decided not to take my teddy bear.

The story continues with Ben constantly changing his mind about whether he will or won't take his bear. In the end he doesn't take it only to discover that Reggie has a teddy bear of his own which he always takes to bed.

Teddy Bear

By Judith Robins

Someone soft and warm
Someone quiet and understanding,
Always willing to listen,
Always willing to play,
Any time of the day,
Always there,
Teddy Bear.

Christopher Robin and Pooh Come to an Enchanted Place, and We Leave Them There

By A. A. Milne

"W here are we going?" said Pooh, hurrying after him, and wondering whether it was to be an Explore or a What-shall-we-do-about-you-know-what.

"No here," said Christopher Robin.

So they began going there, and after they had walked a little way Christopher Robin said:

"What do you like doing best in the world, Pooh?"

"Well," said Pooh, "what I like best – " and then he had to stop and think. Because although eating honey *was* a very good thing to do, there was a moment just before you began to eat it which was better than when you were, but he didn't know what it was called. And then he thought that being with Christopher Robin was a very good thing to do, and having Piglet near was a very friendly thing to have; and so, when he had thought it all out, he said, "What I like best in the whole world is Me and Piglet going to see You, and You saying, 'What about a little something?' and Me saying, 'Well, I shouldn't mind a little something, should you, Piglet,' and it being a hummy sort of day outside, and the birds singing."

"I like that too," said Christopher Robin, "but what I like *doing* best is Nothing."

"How do you do Nothing?" asked Pooh, after he had wondered for a long time.

"Well, it's when people call out at you just as you're going off to do it, What are you going to do, Christopher Robin, and you say, Oh, nothing, and then you go and do it."

"Oh, I see," said Pooh.

"This is a Nothing sort of thing that we're doing now."

"Oh, I see," said Pooh again.

"It means just going along, listening to all the things you can't hear, and not bothering."

"Oh!" said Pooh.

They walked on, thinking of This and That, and by-and-by they came to an enchanted place on the very top of the Forest called Galleons Lap, which is sixty-something trees in a circle; and Christopher Robin knew that it was enchanted because nobody had ever been able to count whether it was sixty-three or sixty-four, not even when he tied a piece of string round each tree after he had counted it. Being enchanted, its floor was not like the floor of the Forest, gorse and bracken and heather, but close-set grass, quiet and smooth and green. It was the only place in the Forest where you could sit down carelessly, without getting up again almost at once and looking for somewhere else. Sitting there they could see the whole world spread out until it reached the sky, and whatever there was all the world over was with them in Galleons Lap.

Suddenly Christopher Robin began to tell Pooh about some of the things: People called Kings and Queens and something called Factors, and a place called Europe, and an island in the middle of the sea where no ships came, and how you make a Suction Pump (if you want to), and when Knights were Knighted, and what comes from Brazil. And Pooh, his back against one of the sixty-something trees, and his paws folded in front of him, said "Oh!" and "I don't know," and thought how wonderful it would be to have a Real Brain which could tell you things. And by-and-by Christopher Robin came to an end of the things, and was silent, and he sat there looking out over the world, and wishing it wouldn't stop.

But Pooh was thinking too, and he said suddenly to Christopher Robin:

"Is it a very Grand thing to be an Afternoon, what you said?"

"A what?" said Christopher Robin lazily, as he listened to something else.

"On a horse," explained Pooh.

"A Knight?"

"Oh, was that it?" said Pooh. "I thought it was a – Is it as Grand as a King and Factors and all the other things you said?"

"Well, it's not as grand as a King," said Christopher Robin, and then, as Pooh seemed disappointed, he added quickly, "but it's grander than Factors."

"Could a Bear be one?"

"Of course he could!" said Christopher Robin. "I'll make you one." And he took a stick and touched Pooh on the shoulder, and said, "Rise, Sir Pooh de Bear, most faithful of all my Knights."

So Pooh rose and sat down and said "Thank you," which is the proper thing to say when you have been made a Knight, and he went into a dream again, in which he and Sir Pump and Sir Brazil and Factors lived together with a horse, and were faithful Knights (all except Factors, who looked after the horse) to Good King Christopher Robin . . . and every now and then he shook his head, and said to himself "I'm not getting it right." Then he began to think of all the things Christopher Robin would want to tell him when he came back from wherever he was going to, and how muddling it would be for a Bear of Very Little Brain to try and get them right in his mind. "So, perhaps," he said sadly to himself, "Christopher Robin won't tell me any more," and he wondered if being a Faithful Knight meant that you just went on being faithful without being told things.

Then, suddenly again, Christopher Robin, who was still looking at the world, with his chin in his hands, called out "Pooh!"

"Yes?" said Pooh.

"When I'm – when — Pooh!"

"Yes, Christopher Robin?"

"I'm not going to do Nothing any more."

"Never again?"

"Well, not so much. They don't let you."

Pooh waited for him to go on, but he was silent again.

"Yes, Christopher Robin?" said Pooh helpfully.

"Pooh, when I'm – *you* know – when I'm *not* doing Nothing, will you come up here sometimes?"

"Just me?"

"Yes, Pooh."

"Will you be here too?"

"Yes, Pooh, I will be, really. I *promise* I will be, Pooh."

"That's good," said Pooh.

"Pooh, *promise* you won't forget about me, ever. Not even when I'm a hundred."

Pooh thought for a little.

"How old shall *I* be then?"

"Ninety-nine."

Pooh nodded.

"I promise," he said.

Still with his eyes on the world, Christopher Robin put out a hand and felt for Pooh's paw.

"Pooh," said Christopher Robin earnestly, "if I – if I'm not quite — " he stopped and tried again – "Pooh, *whatever* happens, you *will* understand, won't you?"

"Understand what?"

"Oh, nothing." He laughed and jumped to his feet. "Come on!"

"Where?" said Pooh.

"Anywhere," said Christopher Robin.

So they went off together. But wherever they go, and whatever happens to them on the way, in that enchanted place on the top of the Forest, a little boy and his Bear will always be playing.

From *The House at Pooh Corner*

Acknowledgements

The editor and publishers gratefully acknowledge permission to reproduce copyright material in this book:

The Teddy Bears by Clara Andrews Williams, 1909, by permission of W. & R. Chambers Ltd; *Me and My Teddy Bear,* author Jack Winters, © 1950 Chappell Music USA/Leo Talent, reproduced by permission of Chappell Music Ltd, London; Bunyip Bluegum's poem from *The Magic Pudding* by Norman Lindsay, © Janet Glad 1918, is reproduced by permission of Angus and Robertson, Publishers; Extract from *Tim Tubby Toes* by Harry Golding, first published in 1913 in the Ward Lock *Little Wonder* series, published by permission of Ward Lock Ltd; *Edward* from *The Best Teddy Bear in the World* by Mrs H. C. Cradock, by permission of Thomas Nelson and Sons Ltd; *Lullaby,* Anon, by permission of House of Nisbet Ltd; *Leaky Ted* © The Estate of Charles Headland, 1988, by permission of Mrs Dorothy Creek; *The Little Brown Bears* by Christine Temple, 1937, by permission of Lutterworth Press Ltd; *Teddy Brown* from *The Brown Family* by Ida Bohatta, translated by June Heard, © Ars Edition AG, Zug, Switzerland; Extracts from *The Enchanted Places* by Christopher Milne, by permission of Methuen, London; *The Auction at Pooh Corner* by E. S. Turner, reproduced by permission of *Punch; The Vain Teddy* by Rose Fyleman, by permission of The Society of Authors as the literary representative of the Estate of Rose Fyleman; *Bibble, Bobble and Bubble* by Josephine Hatcher, published c. 1940 by Hollis and Carter, reproduced by permission of The Bodley Heead; *Night Bears* by Wilma Horsbrugh, by kind permission of the author; extract from *Tidgie's Innings* by V. H. Drummond, by permission of Faber and Faber Ltd; *The Jolly Bear* from *A Bad Child's Book of Moral Verse* by Charlotte Hough, by permission of Faber and Faber Ltd; extract from *Stubbington Manor* by Lady Elizabeth Gorrell, by permission of John Murray (Publishers) Ltd; *Edward George St Clare,* anon, by permission of House of Nisbet Ltd; *Aloysius* (extract from *Brideshead Revisited*) by Evelyn Waugh, reprinted by permission of A. D. Peters and Co. Ltd; *Archie* (extract from *Summoned by Bells*) by Sir John Betjeman, by permission of John Murray (Publishers) Ltd; *Archie and the Strict Baptists* © Sir John Betjeman, reproduced by permission of Curtis Brown Ltd; *The Night Ride* by Aingelda Ardizzone, by permission of the author; *Bears* by Eulia Smith-Zimman, by permission of House of Nisbet Ltd; *A Puzzling Question* from *Something New for a Bear to Do, The Adventures of Mr Manders and Edward James* by Shirley Isherwood, by permission of Century Hutchinson Ltd; Extract from *Bully Bear Goes to a Wedding* by Peter Bull, by permission of Enid Irving; *Bertram Bibblecombe Billyho Bear* © The Estate of Ivy O. Eastwick, by permission of Roger Keen: *Tubby Ted's New Chimney* from *Tubby Ted* by Ursula Hourihane, by permission of Hodder and Stoughton Ltd; *Hóney Bear* by Elizabeth Lang, from her *Book of a Thousand Poems,* by permission of Unwin Hyman; *Teddy Robinson's Night Out* from *The Teddy Robinson Omnibus* by Joan G. Robinson, by permission of Harrap Ltd; *Teddy* © 1988 Brian Hick, by kind permission of the author; *T. R. Arrives* from *Enter T. R.* by Terrance Dicks, by permission of Piccadilly Press Ltd; *Ludvig Bear* by Delma Grant, by permission of the author; *Odd and Elsewhere,* 1971, by James Roose-Evans, by permission of Andre Deutsch Ltd; *King,* © Simon Theobalds 1988, by kind permission of the author; one chapter from *The Shoe Shop Bears* by Margaret J. Baker, reproduced by permission of Curtis Brown Ltd, London; *Bananas,* by permission of Carey Blyton, composer/author; *Teddy Valena* © Brigid Keenan 1988, by kind permission of the author; extract from *Goodnight Ben* by Bernard Waber, 1974, by permission of Hodder and Stoughton Australia Pty Ltd; *Teddy Bear* by Judith Robbins, by permission of House of Nisbet Ltd; extract from Chapter X *The House at Pooh Corner* by A.A. Milne, by permission of Methuen Children's Books, and the Canadian publishers, McClelland and Stewart, Toronto.